The
Home Buying
Game

A Quick and Easy Way to Get the Best Home for Your Money

JULIE GARTON-GOOD

Real Estate Education Company®
a division of Dearborn Financial Publishing, Inc.

This publication is designed to provide accurate and authoritative information in regard to the subject matter covered. It is sold with the understanding that the publisher is not engaged in rendering legal, accounting, or other professional service. If legal advice or other expert assistance is required, the services of a competent professional person should be sought.

Acquisitions Editor: Christine E. Litavsky
Managing Editor: Jack Kiburz
Cover Design: S. Laird Jenkins Corporation
Typesetting: Elizabeth Pitts

Printed in the United States of America

97 98 99 10 9 8 7 6 5 4 3 2 1

Library of Congress Cataloging-in-Publication Data

Garton-Good, Julie.
    The homebuying game : a quick and easy way to get the best home
for your money / Julie Garton-Good.
        p.   cm.
    Includes index.
    ISBN 0-7931-1646-5 (paper)
    1. House buying—United States.   2. Mortgage loans—United States.
I. Title.
HD255.G37   1997
643'.12—dc20   96-36008
                                                                    CIP

Dedication

To my mother, Marion Martin, who taught me that a home is much more than four walls of brick and mortar; and

To my daughter, Crystal Branch, who put up with perpetual moving (as we pyramided our real estate fortune!), countless days at our real estate office and training school (roller-skating in the parking lot), and endless times hearing me say, "Let me make just one more phone call!"

She taught me that wherever she was, I *was* home.

Contents

Step 7   Sharpen Your Pencil   **109**

Step 8   Choose the Best Loan   **132**

Step 9   Pick Up the Keys   **168**

Step 10   Manage Your Castle   **185**

Your Final Move!   **204**

Preface

Hopefully, the book's title caught your eye. But there's a method to our madness. We're calling this book *The Homebuying Game: A Quick and Easy Way to Get the Best Home for Your Money* to convince would-be homebuyers (as well as move-up buyers) that buying a home need not be a frightful, tedious task—particularly if you treat it like playing a game.

The idea came to me after reading the results of a survey conducted by the Federal National Mortgage Association (FNMA—or Fannie Mae). The survey asked consumers to comment on the greatest hurdles they perceived in buying a home. Their primary response? Not knowing how to. They often delayed purchasing because they assumed it was much more difficult than it actually turned out to be!

What better way to simplify the homebuying process than by reducing it to a fun game you can play (and win!). That's why this book is different from others you've seen on homebuying. As with any game, if you play by the rules (one step at a time), master the required challenges, and gather some "aces" along the way, there's no reason you can't win big—and have fun doing it!

Introduction

The Rules of the Game

1. The game has ten easy steps. In each step, you'll draw a series of CHALLENGE CARDS and complete each challenge in turn. If you do,

2. IT'S YOUR MOVE to the next challenge. If you falter,

3. GO TO THE PENALTY BOX. There you'll have additional challenges—but once mastered, you'll receive

4. A TRUMP CARD. Each trump card allows you to continue on to the next step of the Homebuying Game. To win the Homebuying Game you must earn all ten trump cards *in consecutive order.*

Help along the Way

We'll provide assistance to make your homebuying journey a pleasant one. There are KEYS TO SUCCESS, special tips and strategies that will unlock your buying power and tip the odds of winning in your favor.

Be on the lookout for RED FLAGS. They'll alert you to things to check out—especially if they might present a roadblock or cause you to lose money in your homebuying venture.

You'll love and profit from the OH, NO icon, signaling that you've come across an emotional homebuying issue to deal with and master (like paying 100 percent of the asking price just because the apple green carpet reminds you of your childhood).

There you have it—the Homebuying Game. It's easy, fun, and certainly worthwhile. Now, play to win!

Step 1

Check Your Heart!

How Do You Feel about Home Ownership?

A recent survey of 1,857 Americans polled by the Federal National Mortgage Association (FNMA—or Fannie Mae) found that many would-be homebuyers are worried about their ability to raise a down payment and meet monthly mortgage bills.

Fifty-two percent of those polled cited down payments and closing costs as a barrier to home ownership, while 50 percent said having enough income to meet monthly mortgage payments was a hurdle.

Forty-eight percent said they were fearful over job security, and finding the right house in the proper neighborhood was cited by 43 percent.

But when it came to making sacrifices to own a home, 91 percent said they would rather own a home than drive a better car, and 67 percent would put off retirement for ten years in order to obtain one.

Despite the concerns, 61 percent of those polled agreed that now is a good time to buy a home.

How do these survey responses compare to the concerns you have and the sacrifices you would be willing to make to own a home? If you're like a majority of Americans, home ownership is a high priority.

Why, then, is there an element of fear and trepidation in taking the homebuying plunge, and what would make it easier?

Freddie Mac (Federal Home Loan Mortgage Corporation or FHLMC) recently gathered answers from 125 people participating in focus group discussions. The concerns they expressed about homebuying centered around the following:

1. Finding a desirable house in a decent neighborhood
2. Negotiating a fair price
3. Finding trustworthy information on which to base decisions
4. Choosing a mortgage lender and qualifying for an affordable loan
5. Understanding closing costs and the legal commitments of the settlement process

When asked what could help them feel more comfortable about the homebuying process, the participants' responses were specific: They wished the homebuying process was more streamlined, and they wanted more education so that they could feel more comfortable with the process.

Information, education, comfort, feeling good about homebuying—these are the key ingredients in acquiring the American Dream.

That's why your homebuying journey begins with the most logical first step: "The place to start is to check your heart." In this first phase of the Homebuying Game, we'll determine your emotional barometer for owning a home, your level of motivation, as well as your ability to commit to home ownership for the long haul. If you're up to the challenge, draw your first CHALLENGE CARD.

 **Keep Your Homebuying Emotions in Check**

You may be asking, "How do I weigh the pros and cons of buying a home, and how do *I* know if I'm *ready* to be a homeowner?"

Although lots of components enter the picture, my favorite reply is, "You're ready to be a homeowner when you're not only financially but also *emotionally* prepared to handle it!" In fact, the emotional part comes first and is often the overriding factor in choosing which home to buy. Because of that, every time you see this OH NO icon throughout the book, it's your cue to check your emotions to make sure they're in check!

As with many mileposts in life (college, marriage, having kids), homebuying is initially more of an emotional commitment than it is a financial one. Sure, you're parting with thousands of dollars of savings to fund the down payment. And yes, you will be paying hundreds of thousands of dollars in monthly payments over the years. But the bottom line is that most homebuyers purchase first from their emotions, and then "justify" the purchase with their wallets.

Here's an example. You've been looking for a four-bedroom, two-bath home on a large lot for several weeks. While some houses have been okay, you really haven't found *the* house yet.

It's Sunday afternoon and you just happen to pass by a new condo project that's holding an open house. You walk in, fall in love with it, and make a full-price offer on the spot. What happened? Your emotions made the decision for you—pure and simple. The decision was made from your gut, and you justified the purchase with your wallet! Who cares that the condo you chose is "polar" from what you thought you wanted? Your heart and instincts overruled your brain, and you're glad they did!

The same thing happens when a buyer says, "I have to have a formal dining room in my next house." She's not really concerned about a place to put her dining room set and fancy hutch, she's thinking of how great it will feel to have her entire family there for Thanksgiving dinner or how proud she'll feel to see little Johnny sitting in his high chair at the table for his first holiday celebration. Feelings are what homebuyers are after.

But our greatest strengths are also our weaknesses. As you'll see throughout the Homebuying Game, too much emotion is one of the prime reasons why people pay too much for a home, choose a costly mortgage, and fail to maximize home affordability once they do purchase. Strong, overpowering feelings can cause judgments to blur and costs to skyrocket.

One example of costly runaway emotions is the couple who purchased an overpriced home because it had pink carpeting in the bedroom. The wife had grown up in a home where her bedroom was draped and carpeted in Pepto-Bismol pink. In an effort to relive those pleasant childhood memories and feelings, she and her husband went along with all of the financial requirements the seller mandated, including paying the seller's inflated price. Long after the pink carpeting wore out, the buyers were still paying interest on those runaway emotions. (I know this is true—I WAS that homebuyer!)

If you feel you can meet this challenge by understanding that homebuying emotions, while exciting and necessary to the process, are but one part of the homebuying puzzle, IT'S YOUR MOVE ♠

 ## Determine Your Motivation

One of the best tests of a successful homebuying experience is the motivation of the buyer. If you aren't strongly motivated, the disappointments and downturns that can occur during the purchase are likely to devastate you.

But if your motivation is high, you'll be able to rise above the negatives and focus on the end result. It can be an ace in the hole!

What are the most common motivators? They fall into four categories: time pressures, lifestyle changes, emotional situations, and "the fear of loss." (Check to see how *your* motivators rate.)

Time pressures.   This is any event that has a time frame for action such as job relocation, school starting or ending, or an event like the birth of a child. (No woman wants to be moving into a new home when she's nine months pregnant!)

Lifestyle changes.   Empty nesters downsizing into a smaller home when their kids go off to college are a good example of this motivation. (It's common knowledge that you should always sell your large home *before* the kids complete college and move back home!)

Also included in examples of time pressure situations would be divorcing couples and persons moving to a new location for health reasons.

Emotional situations.   A third major motivation, emotional situations, can be one of the most driving, yet volatile. As a real estate broker, I once had a woman call me to list her home. Her husband had recently died and she commented, "I want to buy a smaller place and sell this house. I just can't live here with these memories." After we spent a long time talking and examining her emotions, it was clear to me that listing the house at this time was a bad idea. I told her why I thought she should wait, and she finally agreed. The woman later told me how appreciative she was that I convinced her to wait, and she made it a point to send many referrals my way because of it. Sometimes in emotionally charged situations, the very best thing you can do is nothing!

"Fear of loss."   Of all the motivations, the most interesting one is "the fear of loss." Think back to when you last made a major purchase. You might not have known why you wanted the item, you just didn't want anyone else to get it! That was fear of loss in action. This motivation drives many homebuyers, especially when they know that other buyers are making offers on the home they're considering. In fact, often a house won't have any offers on it for a long time. But as soon as one offer comes in, others appear, as if by magic! Fear of loss was motivating the fence sitters to make an offer. Both need and greed are excellent motivators when it comes to purchasing real estate!

Evaluating the type and level of motivation you have is good. It will help make you a stronger buyer. If you can meet this challenge, then IT'S YOUR MOVE ♣

Evaluate "The Three Cs": Commitment, Credit, Cost

Three benchmarks of a successful homebuyer candidate include the following. See if you're willing to meet these challenges.

Commitment.   In order to clear this hurdle, you must be willing to sacrifice some of those gypsy feelings of freedom moving can afford, commit to spending time on house maintenance and repairs, and be controlled to some degree by the needs of the home (i.e., lawn watering, snow removal, etc.). It's very much like nurturing a child (albeit it one that doesn't talk back nor require college tuition)!

And there may be unhappy times. Like when an obnoxious neighbor makes you wish you could mail the keys to the landlord and move on—but you can't, because you're committed.

Why should you be concerned about home ownership commitment? Because if you live in the home you select for the average time period of seven years, you will have spent more than 2,500 days in it! That's a considerable investment in time, effort, and money.

Credit.   While we'll discuss the finite points of credit in Step #3, it's not too early to face the fact that most homebuyers have to use credit to swing a purchase this large. That means that you'll take on the obligation to check your existing credit picture, or establish one if you haven't done so already, and be willing to manage your credit once the purchase is complete.

The mortgage lender will not be as sympathetic as the landlord about why the payment is late. And even if you do get by with a late house payment here and there, they can mount up to major roadblocks when you want to sell and purchase again.

Dereliction in managing your mortgage and your finances after you purchase a home can result in lost equity, foreclosure, even bankruptcy.

Cost.   You may not have a problem shelling out thousands of dollars of your hard-earned savings for a down payment. And it may not even bother you to pay hundreds of dollars in closing costs. But, unfortunately, those upfront costs of purchase are just the beginning!

You no longer have a landlord to call when the water heater is on the fritz. You'll be alone in the dead of night when the furnace gives up the ghost. And you won't see anyone coming to your rescue with their checkbook when the plumber says, "It took a few hours more time than I thought to repair that leak!"

But if pride of ownership, the tax advantages you'll gain, and the equity you'll build offset your concerns about the three Cs of commitment, credit, and cost, then IT'S YOUR MOVE

Pass the Psychological Homebuyer's Test

Your final challenge in this chapter is to pass the psychological homebuyer's test. I know, no one likes a test. But taking this one could actually save or make you money! And if you pass it, chances are good that your path through the rest of the homebuying process will be a much smoother one. So here goes.

Psychological Homebuyer's Test

If you agree strongly about the item, give it a +1. If you feel neutral about the item, give it a 0. If you feel negative about the item (or if it's outside your capacity), give it a –1.

1. ___ I could live in one location for an extended period of time.
2. ___ I will spend the time required to maintain a home in proper condition.
3. ___ I will establish and maintain a creditworthy lifestyle.
4. ___ I commit to pay my mortgage and home maintenance bills on time.
5. ___ It would not bother me to use my savings to buy a home.
6. ___ I would spend money to keep a home in good repair.
7. ___ I would budget home repair costs into my monthly expenses.
8. ___ I can balance my homebuying emotions with logic and financial ability.
9. ___ I will make sure that the home I buy will address my financial as well as my emotional needs.
10. ___ Pride of home ownership is important to me and a goal I wish to achieve.

SCORING:

If your score is a positive number, then you're a candidate for home ownership. The higher the number, the better the candidate! Congratulations, IT'S YOUR MOVE to Step #2 ⬥

If your test scored a negative number, go back over the questions to determine where you need to focus. For example, questions 1 and 2 deal with Commitment; 3 and 4, building and maintaining Credit; 5, 6, and 7, Costs of ownership; and 8, 9, and 10, Emotions of homebuying. Note: There's nothing wrong with a low score. It just means that homebuying may not fit well into your life at this point. And knowing that fact is half the battle!

If you fail to meet the four CHALLENGE CARD requirements of "Check Your Heart," GO TO THE PENALTY BOX.

Penalty Box

Possible penalties for not addressing your emotions include the following:

1. Feeling tied down to a house you resent
2. Spending unhappy hours on home maintenance and repair
3. Losing your down payment and/or equity if you impulsively sell in haste
4. Damaging your credit if you default on your loan and/or walk away from your investment altogether

For "help" out of the PENALTY BOX:

1. Work on improving the three Cs of commitment, credit, and cost.
2. Express your concerns about homebuying with someone you know who has had a positive experience. Did they have similar reservations initially? How did they overcome them?
3. Consider purchasing a home when it's more mentally appropriate for you. Timing is critical for successful, long-term homeownership.
4. Perhaps consider purchasing with a cobuyer. This could take some of the financial and emotional pressure off you initially. (But be as sure as you can that it's the *right* cobuyer!)

 Take Trump Card #1

Controlling your emotions when buying a home is imperative. It allows you to have a stronger negotiating position with the seller (you won't be showing your hand!) and you'll be able to focus on evaluating the purchase logically—with your head. (Remember my expensive Pepto-Bismol pink carpeting story!)

Step 2

Watch Your Timing

Put Timing on Your Side

After you've determined that you can handle the emotional tensions of homebuying, it's merely a matter of time, or timing, that you need to focus on. As with any major purchase and life-style change, timing can be critical. And given that you'll be spending thousands of dollars on this homebuying decision, improper timing can hit you right in the wallet!

Contrary to popular belief, renting at times makes more sense than purchasing. Granted, it may not be the most emotionally comfortable alternative, but financially it may make more sense.

Here are the timing challenges to tackle before you start your home purchase. Draw your card.

Look into the Crystal Ball of Your Future

If you could look into a crystal ball, what would your short-term future hold? Are there indicators that may signal a change in your living environment, such as a job relocation?

In the following example of homebuying gone awry, the Johnsons should have looked into their crystal ball before purchasing their first home.

Jim and Laurie Johnson have been married for three years and want to purchase their first home. Mr. Johnson is a district sales manager for a software company and is next in line for a promotion that could include relocation. Mrs. Johnson is a self-employed graphic artist.

They have saved enough money for a 10 percent down payment on a conventional loan (plus closing costs). They've eyed a $100,000 house that's one-of-a-kind. Although it is a bit overimproved and the most expensive house in the neighborhood, the Johnsons *must* have it. So they buy it and move in.

Six months go by. Jim receives word that his promotion has come through and that they will be moving out of state. The Johnsons call a real estate agent to list the house. But when the agent does the comparative market analysis (a CMA) to determine what they can sell it for, she finds that they overpaid for the house. The problem compounds because the market has softened and $96,000 will be the most they can expect to get for the property, even including the improvements they've made.

But the biggest blow comes when the agent calculates the Johnsons' sales costs. Even if the property sells for the full listed price, after paying off their $90,000 mortgage, the sales commission, and closing expenses, they will need to *bring money* to the closing in order to sell! Ouch! Their dream home purchase has become a nightmare sale!

While it's illogical that families who relocate should never purchase a home, potentially any short-term ownership causes special considerations.

What could the Johnsons have done differently? The obvious changes would be to purchase a home on the lower price side of the market, not overpay for the property, and definitely not buy an overimproved house. These factors signal money lost at purchase, resulting in even greater losses at resale. (Later, in Step #6, we'll cover how to best choose a neighborhood and evaluate a property.)

Knowing that relocation was a possibility, the Johnsons might have gone with an assumable loan. With competitive interest rates, an assumable loan could add to the property's marketability and save the parties time and money, sidestepping new financing.

And since Jim was next in line for a promotion that could include relocation, holding off on their purchase might have made more financial sense.

Although all circumstances are different, the Johnsons' combination of short-term ownership, unpredictable housing market trends, and high selling costs are not unusual. Sadder still is the fact that the Johnsons had to save for three years to accumulate their $10,000 down payment. Now it's gone. And it's likely to be three or more years before they can purchase again! When they do buy again, it may cost them more to obtain the house they want.

As you can see, timing your purchase based on what's happening in your life can mean the difference between sweet success and financial disaster. If you can meet this challenge with relative certainty, IT'S YOUR MOVE ✦

 ## Pencil Out the Financial Pros and Cons of Buying vs. Renting

A recent survey conducted by the National Association of REALTORS® noted that tax benefits are one of the major reasons people become homeowners. You'll have property taxes to deduct, not to mention a bucket of mortgage interest each year. And if you've never itemized deductions on your income tax return, being a homeowner will change that picture.

Once the equity in your property grows and you decide to take out a second mortgage or equity loan, you can deduct interest on up to $100,000 of that, too.

And benefits abound when you decide to sell your castle. If you replace your home with another of equal or greater value within a period of two years before or after the sale of the home, tax on the profit you make is postponed indefinitely. This replacement process can occur as many times as you desire. And once either you or your spouse reaches age 55, you are entitled to a one-time $125,000 tax break free from federal taxes on all previous profit you've made buying and selling homes you've owned. What a deal!

But to get to the goodies, you've got to first plunk down money for closing and then keep plunking down cash as you go. It's all of the little monthly extras that add up to hefty financial responsibility when you purchase a home. Unfortunately, if you're living hand-to-mouth in a rental unit, home ownership is likely to be even more strapping. Maintenance, repair costs, and increased property taxes can put stress on you, especially if these costs aren't anticipated and planned for in a monthly budget.

Here's an example. Susan Stratton purchased her first home and is pleased that her mortgage payment is just slightly higher than the rent she paid for several years. But are her costs really equal? She's added the costs of home insurance, condo fees, and monthly payments for the washer and dryer she needed. In addition, she is paying off her credit card for draperies she charged plus the large car payment and three other credit card payments she was already making. Since she used all of her savings for the down payment and closing costs, she has no backup source of funds.

Although it's true that she is now investing in her long-term future and a quality lifestyle (plus the advantage of tax benefits for home ownership), the reality is that if Susan can't balance her finances in the early months, she could find herself strapped to make her mortgage payment.

After only four months as a homeowner, that's just how Susan feels! The water heater sprung a leak not long after closing and needed repair. Then the condo association raised the monthly maintenance fee, and the air-conditioning unit began whirring, requiring a service call. If Susan can't work extra overtime, she will be short making her mortgage payment for the month—not the joyful feeling of homeownership she expected!

What could Susan have done differently? First of all, she could have budgeted for the unknown. I know, nothing in life is guaranteed. But unless you anticipate costs over and above what you spent as a renter, you are being grossly unrealistic as a homeowner.

Second, Susan might have chosen a loan that did not require using all of her savings for the down payment and closing costs.

She would then have a slush fund to fall back on for initial emergency repairs until she could accumulate a reserve account.

The most important thing that Susan could have done differently was to hold off adding any new debt after she purchased. This *was* within her control and would have given her time to adjust financially and mentally to the new costs she faced.

I've met several first-time buyers who declare a credit card moratorium for several months to a year after purchasing their first home. Anticipating that they'd need time to get used to new and unsuspected financial obligations, they waited to add new debt until they were comfortable. Wise buyers taking a wise tack.

You might suggest that Susan should have waited until her revolving debt was lower before she bought a home. While it might have helped Susan balance her short-term financial picture, waiting to purchase could have cost her more money, as we'll see later in this Step.

If you've penciled out the initial pros and cons of buying versus renting as they fit your situation, then IT'S YOUR MOVE ♣

 ## Determine Whether a Large Cash Outlay Is Pending

This challenge card may seem like a simple one: if you need money for another major purchase, evaluate how much of your savings you should use for your home and/or if making both purchases is wise at this time.

Buyers who don't plan for major multiple cash outlays find themselves financially and mentally stressed, not enjoying either purchase.

Don't forget that even if you can borrow money to fund the second purchase, you should consider the price you'll have to pay for that money. Funding large items from high-interest credit cards may not be the wisest financial or emotional route to take. But it's important to decide this before you part with your savings.

If no large cash outlay is pending (or you've provided for it), then IT'S YOUR MOVE ♣

Take a Look at Your Employment Picture

It's said that the number one fear potential homebuyers face is that of unemployment. In fact, it's also the major reason why repeat buyers hesitate about buying up to a larger or more expensive home. If your job is precarious, it's tough to justify funding more debt.

But the reason we haven't tackled this challenge earlier is that it's really not the major concern it initially appears to be. I'm not advocating that you rush right out and buy a house if you know you're going to be unemployed in the near future. (In fact, it probably won't work. During the financing process, the lender will uncover the facts when your employment, its continuation or lack thereof, is verified!) But other than impending long-term unemployment, the fear of being temporarily out of a job should have little effect on whether or not you purchase a home.

Here's why. Becoming unemployed is one of those events in life that you have very little control over (most of the time). If it happens, you make the best of it.

Second, you were probably going to pay to live somewhere anyway, weren't you? Why not make those payments for something you'll enjoy and build equity in?

Third, if you don't purchase and are laid off, it will take you a certain period of time to re-establish your work history once you do find employment again, perhaps as long as two years. And if the job you later find pays less, you won't be able to qualify for as much house as you could right now.

Fourth, if you purchase now and are laid off, the equity in your home could serve as financial padding if you need it. Lenders have been known to make equity loans based primarily on the property value, not on the borrower's employment status. A small equity loan might make the difference between peace of mind and financial ruin.

If you're postponing homebuying for fear of losing your job, make sure your concern is based on facts, not perceptions. And that your decision does not sacrifice short-term peace of mind for long-term financial gain. If you're not going to be a worry wart about losing your job and will consider it just one part of the homebuying puzzle, IT'S YOUR MOVE ♣

How Do the Local Economy and Current Housing Market Affect Your Decision?

While a lackluster local economy won't inevitably stand in the way of your home purchase, it can have an effect on how much you pay for the house and how your home investment performs in the short run.

If homes are in low supply but demand is high, it may cost you top dollar to get what you want. This is called a *seller's market,* and it can be caused when local development and growth are constricted, or the supply of existing resale housing and/or new construction can't keep pace with demand. But the good news is that once you buy a house under these circumstances, you're now on the winning side as a potential seller. If demand continues, property values should remain stable and perhaps appreciate.

In a *buyer's market,* the reverse is true. There's an abundance of housing with little demand. A glut of sellers chase too few buyers, resulting in price cutting and eroding values. While it's good news that you may pay less for the property, the gain can be offset by low equity buildup and appreciation in the early years of ownership.

How can you tell if a market is favorable for purchasing and best protect yourself in the process? We'll cover this in greater depth in Step #4, but here are some basics to help you decide.

In a seller's market, make sure you aren't overpaying for the property. Just as the Johnsons found in our earlier scenario, you set the stage for potential financial loss if you pay too much (especially when you hold the house for a short term).

 Try to negotiate other items with the sellers, like having them pick up more closing costs. They can "win" by getting their price, while you limit the amount of cash you bring to closing.

Last, don't let too few properties on the market pressure you into buying. Remember that fear of loss can falsely motivate buyers, especially if they feel that there's not much to choose from. Be methodical in your purchase and realize that even though you want to buy, making a bad decision is far worse than losing a house to another buyer.

If you are in a buyer's market, you may feel like a kid in a candy store—so much to chose from and better negotiating power with sellers. But the caution is not how low the price you pay for the property, but how long you'll hold onto it when you do.

The Johnsons' plight shows us another lesson. Holding a property for a short term in a buyer's market may mean that equity won't build up at a satisfactory speed, leaving you high and dry to pay closing costs if you have to sell. The key: be sure to buy in a neighborhood with strong property values, perhaps use a bit more down payment, and evaluate up front how long you'll keep the property.

Major layoffs in an area's employment market can affect the value of housing. In today's world of corporate restructuring, a good buy on a three-bedroom house on Monday can become a noncompetitive price or even a bad price on Friday when numerous other three-bedroom houses are added to the market due to layoffs. Using the facts we previously covered about a buyer's market, you can negotiate a good price while being aware that until inventory has diminished, sale prices may remain flat or even drop. You would be wise to hold off purchasing until market prices are at their lowest point.

After you've evaluated buyers' vs. sellers' markets, you're ready to take another challenge in this Step—determining how much it may cost you if you wait to buy. IT'S YOUR MOVE

 ## Evaluate the True Cost of Waiting

How many times have you heard a potential homebuyer say, "I'm waiting for the interest rates to come down before I buy"? That person may not be saving money, but actually costing himself additional funds by waiting!

So before you can decide if waiting to buy makes good economic sense for you, put yourself in this real-world example to weigh the options.

You want to buy a home that costs $100,000, but are considering waiting because you believe that interest rates might fall in the next year. (We'd love to borrow your crystal ball!)

If you did wait one year to purchase and interest rates did fall .5 percent, say, from 8.5 percent to 8 percent, you would have saved $11.69 per month on your monthly payments for your 90 percent loan.

But would you really save? The house that was $100,000 last year is now $103,000 (based on a nominal annual inflation rate of

3 percent.) And even with savings of $11.69 per month, it would take you 21 years to recoup that $3,000 additional cost, not to mention the additional interest you'd pay on the larger loan amount!

And that's not all. A larger loan could mean more closing costs, changes in underwriting guidelines could make it tougher to get a loan, and the house you wanted might not be available. Lots of chances to take for virtually no real savings.

Remember one last point. Growing equity in a home is one of the only savings vehicles available for Americans today. Just as inflation increased the purchase price in our example over a one-year period, time can increase your equity as well through inflation, supply and demand, and market conditions. So the house with a market value of $100,000 today, $103,000 next year, and $106,390 in two years (factoring in inflation at a meager 3 percent) is quietly compounding your investment. But there's one catch—you have to purchase first!

If you've tackled the previous challenges, you're ready for the final one in this Step—IT'S YOUR MOVE

Pass the Financial Homebuyer's Test

Financial Homebuyer's Test

If you agree strongly about the item, give it a +1. If you feel neutral about the item, give it a zero. If you feel negative about the item (or if it's outside your capacity), give it a –1.

1. ___ It appears that I will own the home long enough to sidestep any short-term loss.
2. ___ If I purchase a one-of-a-kind house, I know that I may need to hold it longer in order to sell and make a profit.
3. ___ I have a current household budget and believe that my current debt picture is stable enough to add a mortgage payment and not be strapped.

4. ___ I am willing to commit something monthly to a household emergency fund. I will impound $_____ per month.

5. ___ If necessary, I am willing to commit to a new debt moratorium after I get the house in order to balance my budget.

6. ___ I have projected other large cash outlays for things I may need in the coming months and feel that I can financially handle buying a house at this time.

7. ___ I am realistic about my continued employment and believe that now is the best time for me to buy a home.

8. ___ If it becomes necessary for me to free up cash using my equity, I will do so prudently, treating my equity like a long-term savings account.

9. ___ I understand how buying in either a seller's or a buyer's market can affect my purchase and will carefully evaluate the property and negotiate the best purchase before I buy.

10. ___ I have evaluated the cost of waiting and agree that buying now is in my best economic interest.

Scoring

If your score is a positive number, then you're a candidate for home ownership. The higher the number, the better the candidate! Congratulations, IT'S YOUR MOVE to Step #3

If it's a negative number, go back over the questions to determine where you need to focus. For example, questions 1 and 2 deal with what's happening in your immediate future, questions 3, 4, and 5 deal with budgeting, question 6 focuses on other large cash outlays, questions 7 and 8 on your employment and tapping your equity, question 9 on evaluating market conditions, and question 10 on the economic side of waiting to purchase. Note: There's nothing wrong with a low score. It just means that homebuying may not fit well into your financial picture at this time. Work on the areas pinpointed, and you'll soon be ready to buy!

If you fail to meet the seven CHALLENGE CARD requirements of "Check Your Timing," GO TO THE PENALTY BOX.

Penalty Box

Possible penalties for improper timing of your home purchase could include the following:

1. Losing your down payment and equity when you sell the house after short-term ownership (and/or having to bring a check to closing to sell!)
2. Sleepless nights wondering how you're going to meet your mortgage payment because your debt is overloaded
3. Paying too much for your house in a seller's market, or buying a house with low appreciation in a buyer's market
4. Waiting to buy only to find that you lose your employment or can't qualify for the loan you need

For "help" out of the PENALTY BOX:

1. Be realistic about your current budget and your ability to budget. Talk to your accountant or other financial adviser if you have doubts about handling your current debt load plus a mortgage payment. Uneasiness now will only escalate if you're financially overburdened.
2. Be realistic about how long you'll keep the property. If you're a growing family, the three years you anticipate may be only several months when an extra bedroom is needed. Try to project whether the property you're purchasing will give you some future flexibility. If not, you may lose money when you sell too soon.
3. If you do decide to wait before you purchase a home, make sure it's for the right reasons. Make a game plan for what will need to happen before you buy and a time frame for making it happen. Then you'll know when you've reached that goal and decision making will be easier.

Take Trump Card #2

Your best play is to briefly evaluate what's happening in your employment and immediate future, and then make your move to home ownership. In general, waiting to buy a home can end up costing you money!

Step 3

Look in Your Wallet

Look in Your Wallet (before the Lender Does!)

You've heard the adage "Prepare in advance of need." This has great relevance in laying the proper financial foundation for buying a house. And unless you take the necessary steps in order (check your credit, visit the lender, find the property), you're more likely to be denied the loan or end up paying much more than you needed to because of it.

Don't Put the Cart before the Horse

Hopefully you haven't looked for property before reading this chapter. Why? Because it can be the homebuyer's kiss of death to find the house you want before you look in your wallet.

You may have a pretty good idea of the size of the mortgage payment you can comfortably pay. But it goes much deeper than that. And unless you take these first few steps of homebuying in the order we're going to enumerate, you may suffer dire consequences, including a shortage of money for the down payment, a credit glitch—even having to walk away from a house you've fallen in love with!

Here's an example of what happens if the homebuying steps aren't taken in proper sequence. Prospective buyers Rod and Rachel Holman are skimming the home ads in the paper and get excited about one they see advertised. This one happens to be for sale by owner (FSBO). They call, rush over to view the property, and end up making an offer on the spot for exactly what the seller wanted. I mean, after all, they "*love* the house and just have to have it!"

They give the seller a check for $1,000 with the offer and tell her that they'll be going to the lender on Monday morning.

The visit to the lender is anything but joyous. Not only are they informed that they've committed to buy a house $10,000 over what they can afford, but the amount they have available for the down payment and closing costs is only enough for a house priced $20,000 less. Houdini couldn't get them into the house they want!

The crowning blow comes when they call the seller back, only to find out that they did not make qualifying for a loan a contingency of the offer. They end up losing their $1,000 earnest money, a substantial part of the down payment they've been saving.

Have we got your attention? Good, because if you approach the steps of your home purchase from the angle we're going to describe, you'll have fewer disappointments and will be more rationally prepared to make a sound financial decision when you do find that "have-to-have" home.

 ## Vow to Tackle the Homebuying Steps in the Proper Order

The primary steps of homebuying are easy. First, organize your finances and check your credit. Second, see a lender. Third, find a real estate professional to work with. And fourth, locate the house.

You may be thinking, "This is impossible! I can't be patient like this. I have to look at houses in order to get emotionally charged up about house hunting." This is fine if you can pay cash and are not concerned about securing financing. But because most of us don't have this luxury, being grounded enough now to pull your financial information together will be important. That's why it's best done in advance of need and before homebuying emotions take you on a roller-coaster ride. Slighting this three-step process now could mean delaying the close of your purchase later and put extra stress on you once the loan application is made.

Trust me. Follow the steps and the process will be much more streamlined and satisfying. Just as in stud poker when you're dealt an ace face down, not to be exposed until the showdown, this approach can be your ace in the hole! Do I have your solemn promise that we'll stay on course together? Good! Then IT'S YOUR MOVE

 ## Analyze Your Assets

This is a simple challenge. List all of your assets just as on Figure 3.1, Asset Worksheet.

Why is this necessary? Not only does the lender want to see the value of what you own, it shows a pattern of how well you've accumulated assets and where you've placed your financial priorities.

I once heard a lender ask a man why he hadn't purchased a home previously or saved more in cash over the years from his somewhat substantial income. He replied by showing the lender titles to three boats, all of which were free and clear. He was spending his money on something he enjoyed. Those assets not only showed the lender where the money had gone, but also that the applicant was able to pay off debt over time and accumulate substantial assets.

The key is: when in doubt, list it. There's no such thing as being too strong financially as a buyer, but the contrary is certainly true.

Assets include other real estate you own, personal property, financial instruments such as CDs, stocks, and bonds, as well as your savings and checking account balances.

In addition to stating where the accounts are held, be sure to have the actual account numbers on hand. The lender will require these at the time of application.

FIGURE 3.1   Asset Worksheet

Description	Cash or Market Value
Cash deposit toward purchases held by:	$
List checking and savings accounts below	
Name and address of Bank, S&L, or Credit Union	
Acct. no.	$
Name and address of Bank, S&L, or Credit Union	
Acct. no.	$
Name and address of Bank, S&L, or Credit Union	
Acct. no.	$
Name and address of Bank, S&L, or Credit Union	
Acct. no.	$
Stocks & Bonds (Company name/number & description)	$
Life Insurance net cash value Face amount: $	$
Subtotal Liquid Assets	**$**
Real Estate owned (enter market value from schedule of real estate owned)	$
Vested interest in retirement fund	$
Net worth of business(es) owned (attach financial statement)	$
Automobiles owned (make and year)	$
Other Assets (itemize)	$
Total Assets	**$**

If you'll be purchasing with a coborrower, make sure he or she completes a list of assets, too. Once you've done this, IT'S YOUR MOVE ♣

 ### Decipher Your Debts

For many buyers, this is the least pleasing activity, but a necessary evil. Now's the time to list them on the Debt/Liabilities Worksheet (Figure 3.2). And we'll help you by sorting them out in stages, based on debt type.

Step 1—Current living expense: mortgages you owe or rent you pay. If you currently make a mortgage payment, you'll need to find your payment book for information on the loan number, the amount of the payments, the approximate balance on the loan, and the address where you make the payments. You also need to know if your payment includes taxes and insurance. If it doesn't, how much are they and when are they paid (e.g., semiannually)?

If you are currently renting, you'll need to note the amount of the rent, if you're on a lease or month to month, how long you've been renting, the name of the landlord, and where the payments are made.

Whether you're an owner or a renter, you'll need to provide the lender with a two-year history of where you've lived.

Step 2—Installment loan debt. Installment debts are those which are paid back in a series of payments. One example that we're all familiar with is the installment car payment.

You'll need to jot down the monthly payments, the approximate outstanding balance on the loan, and how many payments you have remaining. (You'll soon see why this latter information is important.) Be sure to note a loan or reference number, as well as where the payments are made.

Step 3—Revolving debt. Think of revolving debt as obligations that keep coming around—just like a revolving door! These include obligations that bill every 30 days such as MasterCard, Visa, American Express, Diner's Club, and Discover cards, as

FIGURE 3.2 Debt/Liabilities Worksheet

	Monthly Payment Months Left to Pay	Unpaid Balance
Name and address of Company	$ Payment/Mos.	$
Acct. no.		
Name and address of Company	$ Payment/Mos.	$
Acct. no.		
Name and address of Company	$ Payment/Mos.	$
Acct. no.		
Name and address of Company	$ Payment/Mos.	$
Acct. no.		
Name and address of Company	$ Payment/Mos.	$
Acct. no.		
Name and address of Company	$ Payment/Mos.	$
Acct. no.		
Name and address of Company	$ Payment/Mos.	$
Acct. no.		
Alimony/Child Support/ Separate Maintenance Payments Owed to:	$	
Job-Related Expense (child care, union dues, etc.)	$	
Total Monthly Payments	$	

well as department store and catalog companies. As before, you need the current amount you owe, the monthly amount you pay, the credit card number, and the location where you send your payments.

Step 4—Other debt (e.g., child support, alimony, student loans). As with assets, when in doubt, spell it out. Let the lender decide if it's important at the time of application. All you're trying to do now is list the debt, the account or reference number, approximately how much it is, and where you make the payments.

Don't forget debts that you owe but perhaps are not making payments on yet, such as deferred student loans. These amounts can figure into your debt picture for loan qualifying, so don't forget to mention them. Once you've tallied up your debts, IT'S YOUR MOVE ♣

 ## Complete the Worksheet to Determine How Much House You Can Afford

We'll explore how the lender takes bits and pieces of the information you've gathered and uses them to determine the loan amount for which you can qualify. But now that you've gathered the information yourself, you can use it to do a thumbnail determination of what you can afford.

Filling in the Quick Qualify Form

Use Figure 3.3 to understand "What Can You Afford?" Grab a pencil and we'll work through the form together so that you can plug in your specific information. (Note: This form reflects guidelines used to qualify a borrower for a conventional loan. FHA, VA, and other loan qualifying formats can vary, particularly in the qualifying ratios used.)

Step 1.   Post the amount of your annual gross income in Column A and then divide it by 12 to determine your monthly gross income. Post that answer in Column B as well.

Step 2.   The form states that "lenders will allow 28 percent of monthly gross income for housing expense." So in Column B, multiply your monthly gross income by 28 percent and post your answer on the line provided. This represents the maximum monthly housing expense (principal, interest, taxes, and insurance) for which you can qualify.

Step 3.   The form states that "many lenders allow 36 percent of monthly gross income for long-term debt." So multiply your gross monthly income by 36 percent and post that answer in Column A. This represents the maximum amount of your monthly

FIGURE 3.3   What Can You Afford?

	Column A	Column B
Annual gross income	$ 164400	
Divide by number of months	÷ 12	
Monthly gross income (Record it in both columns. Perform operations only on figures in the same vertical column.)	= 13700	= 13700
Lenders will allow 28% of monthly gross income for housing expense.		× .28
Maximum monthly housing expense allowance (Column B)		= 3836
Many lenders allow 36% of monthly gross income for long-term debt.	× .36	
Long-term monthly expense allowance	= 4932	
Figure out your monthly long-term obligations below, and subtract the total from the allowance:	− 610	

child support.............$	
auto loan ....+	410.00
credit cards ....+	200.00
other ....+	
other ....+	
total long-term obligations ..=	610.00

	Column A	Column B
Monthly housing expense allowance	= 4322	
Look at the last amount in Columns A and B above. Record the smaller amount.	$ 3836	
About 20% of the housing expense allowance is for taxes and insurance, leaving 80% for payment of mortgage (principal and interest)	× .80	
Allowable monthly principal and interest (PI) expense	= 3068.80	
Divide this amount by the appropriate monthly payment factor.	÷ .0073376 8% @ 30 yr = 418.00	
Multiply by 1,000	× 1,000	
Affordable mortgage amount (what the lender will lend)	$ 418000	

income that can go toward your long-term debt, which includes your housing expense plus debts that can't be paid off in ten months (or are recurring.)

Step 4.   Next comes the fun part. Tally up your long-term obligations (any debt that can't be paid off in ten months or is recurring in nature such as child support, auto loans, credit cards, etc.) and *subtract* them from the previous answer in Column A. This answer will be posted as your "monthly housing expense allowance" in Column A.

Step 5.   This step asks you to look at the last amounts in Columns A and B and "record the smaller amount." The lender goes with the smaller amount to compensate for the amount of debt the borrower has.

Step 6.   The form considers that you don't yet know exactly what your property taxes and insurance are (since you haven't found *the* house)—so we're estimating that approximately 20 percent of the housing expense allowance is for taxes and insurance, leaving 80 percent for mortgage principal and interest. Multiply your previous answer by 80 percent to find this amount.

Step 7.   Next, look at the amortization table (see Figure 3.4). Based on current interest rates in your area, find the monthly payment factor that corresponds to the interest rate and divide it into the last answer you found in Column A. (Example: $900 divided by .0073376, which is the factor for 8 percent interest for a 30-year loan term, gives you 122.655.)

Step 8.   Multiply your last answer by 1,000, because the chart represents principal and interest for each $1,000 of loan amount. (Example: 122.655 × 1,000 = $122,655)
    You can afford this much loan!

How to Analyze Your Findings

What did we just do? Simply, we tallied up our annual gross income, divided it into monthly income, applied the qualifying ratios of 28 percent for housing expense and 36 percent for total

FIGURE 3.4   Amortization Factors

To determine the monthly P and I (principal and interest) payment:
1. Locate the factor for the desired interest rate and term.
2. Multiply this rate/term factor by the loan amount.

To determine the principal amount of the loan:
1. Locate the factor for the desired interest rate and term.
2. Divide the monthly P and I payment by this rate/term factor.

Term in Years	INTEREST RATE					
	6%	6¼%	6½%	6¾%	7%	7¼%
5	.0193328	.0194490	.0195661	.0196835	.0198012	.0199193
8	.0131414	.0132640	.0133862	.0135096	.0136337	.0137585
10	.0111021	.0112280	.0113548	.0114824	.0116108	.0177401
12	.0097585	.0098880	.0100192	.0101510	.0102838	.0104176
15	.0084386	.0085740	.0087111	.0088491	.0089883	.0091286
18	.0075816	.0077230	.0078656	.0080096	.0081550	.0083017
20	.0071643	.0073093	.0074557	.0076036	.0077530	.0079038
25	.0064430	.0065970	.0067521	.0069091	.0070680	.0072281
30	.0059955	.0061570	.0063207	.0064860	.0066530	.0068218
35	.0057019	.0058710	.0060415	.0062142	.0063886	.0065647
40	.0055021	.0056770	.0058546	.0060336	.0062143	.0063967

Term in Years	INTEREST RATE					
	7½%	7¾%	8%	8¼%	8½%	8¾%
5	.0200379	.0201570	.0202764	.0203963	.0205165	.0206372
8	.0138838	.0140099	.0141367	.0142640	.0143921	.0145208
10	.0118702	.0120010	.0121328	.0122653	.0123986	.0125327
12	.0105523	.0106879	.0108245	.0109620	.0111006	.0112400
15	.0092701	.0094128	.0095565	.0097014	.0098479	.0099949
18	.0084497	.0085990	.0087496	.0089015	.0090546	.0092089
20	.0080593	.0082095	.0083644	.0085207	.0086782	.0088371
25	.0073899	.0075533	.0077182	.0078845	.0080523	.0082214
30	.0069921	.0071641	.0073376	.0075127	.0076891	.0078670
35	.0067424	.0069218	.0071026	.0072849	.0074686	.0076536
40	.0065807	.0067662	.0069531	.0071414	.0073309	.0075217

FIGURE 3.4   Amortization Factors (Continued)

Term in Years	INTEREST RATE					
	9%	9¼%	9½%	9¾%	10%	10¼%
5	.0207584	.0208799	.0210019	.0211243	.0212471	.0213703
8	.0146502	.0147802	.0149109	.0150423	.0151742	.0153068
10	.0126676	.0128033	.0129398	.0130771	.0132151	.0133540
12	.0113803	.0115216	.0116637	.0118069	.0119508	.0120957
15	.0101427	.0102919	.0104422	.0105937	.0107461	.0108996
18	.0093644	.0095212	.0096791	.0098382	.0099984	.0101598
20	.0089972	.0091587	.0093213	.0094852	.0096503	.0098165
25	.0083920	.0085638	.0087370	.0089114	.0090871	.0092639
30	.0080462	.0082268	.0084085	.0085916	.0087758	.0089611
35	.0078399	.0080274	.0082161	.0084059	.0085967	.0087886
40	.0077136	.0079066	.0081006	.0082956	.0084916	.0086882

Term in Years	INTEREST RATE					
	10½%	10¾%	11%	11¼%	11½%	11¾%
5	.0214940	.0216180	.0217425	.0218674	.0219927	.0221184
8	.0154401	.0155740	.0157085	.0158436	.0159794	.0161158
10	.0134935	.0136339	.0137751	.0139169	.0140596	.0142030
12	.0122415	.0123881	.0125356	.0126840	.0128332	.0129833
15	.0110540	.0112095	.0113660	.0115235	.0116819	.0118414
18	.0103223	.0104859	.0106505	.0108162	.0109830	.0111507
20	.0099838	.0101523	.0103219	.0104926	.0106643	.0108371
25	.0094419	.0096210	.0098012	.0099824	.0101647	.0103480
30	.0091474	.0093349	.0095233	.0097127	.0099030	.0100941
35	.0089813	.0091750	.0093696	.0095649	.0097611	.0099579
40	.0088857	.0090840	.0092829	.0094826	.0096828	.0098836

Term in Years	INTEREST RATE					
	12%	12¼%	12½%	12¾%	13%	13¼%
5	.0222445	.0223710	.0224980	.0226254	.0227531	.0228813
8	.0162529	.0163906	.0165289	.0166678	.0168073	.0169475
10	.0143471	.0144920	.0146377	.0147840	.0149311	.0150789
12	.0131342	.0132860	.0134386	.0135921	.0137463	.0139014
15	.0120017	.0121630	.0123523	.0124884	.0126525	.0128174
18	.0113195	.0114892	.0116600	.0118317	.0120043	.0121779
20	.0110109	.0111857	.0113615	.0115382	.0117158	.0118944
25	.0105323	.0107175	.0109036	.0110906	.0112784	.0114671
30	.0102862	.0104790	.0106726	.0108670	.0110620	.0112578
35	.0101555	.0103537	.0105525	.0107519	.0109520	.0111524
40	.0100850	.0102869	.0104892	.0106919	.0108951	.0110987

FIGURE 3.4   Amortization Factors (Continued)

Term in Years	INTEREST RATE					
	13½%	13¾%	14%	14¼%	14½%	14¾%
5	.0230099	.0231389	.0232683	.0233981	.0235283	.0236590
8	.0170882	.0172296	.0173716	.0175141	.0176573	.0178011
10	.0152275	.0153767	.0155267	.0156774	.0158287	.0159808
12	.0140572	.0142139	.0143713	.0145295	.0146885	.0148483
15	.0129832	.0131499	.0133175	.0134858	.0136551	.0138251
18	.0123523	.0125276	.0127038	.0128809	.0130587	.0132374
20	.0120738	.0122541	.0124353	.0126172	.0128000	.0129836
25	.0116565	.0118467	.0120377	.0122293	.0124217	.0126147
30	.0114542	.0116512	.0118486	.0120469	.0122456	.0124448
35	.0113534	.0115548	.0117567	.0119590	.0121617	.0123647
40	.0113026	.0115069	.0117114	.0119162	.0121213	.0123267

long-term debt, and subtracted our monthly debt, with the remainder left over being the maximum house payment we could afford! The ratios we used can change based on the type of loan you choose as well as the lender you use.

Remember that the worksheet lets you calculate the maximum *loan* you can qualify for—not the maximum house you can afford. Be sure to take the amount of your down payment into consideration when determining this.

The form you just completed is designed to give you a rough idea of how much house payment you can afford. Be careful not to take it too literally, though, since a good mortgage lender can apply other information (called compensating factors) that may contribute additional positives to your qualifying profile. That's why it's vital that you be prequalified or preapproved with a lender *before* tackling the househunting step.

Conversely, you can have a strong qualifying profile, but adverse credit may block you. It's the positive combination of many underwriting factors that will cinch the loan for you.

Calculating Your Ratios

Our calculations on the form were merely to determine the maximum amount of loan we could obtain. But what if you already know that, but want to know if you make enough money to afford it? In other words, you want to know what *your* ratios are!

All you have to do is back up through the process we just took. For example, our $122,655 loan required a monthly principal and interest payment of $900. To that amount, we'd need to add back the 20 percent we took out for taxes and insurance. So our maximum PITI (principal, interest, taxes, insurance) payment would be $1,080.

What amount of monthly income would we need in order to qualify for that payment? Let's use the standard qualifying ratios to find out. We'll *divide* $1,080 by 28 percent. This equals $3,857.14. That's the amount of monthly income we'd need to qualify for a $1,080 PITI payment.

Let's say instead we had $4,200 in monthly income. What would our housing ratio be then? To find it, we'd divide the $1,080 payment by the $4,200 monthly income. The answer (and the ratio) is 26. This means that only 26 percent of our monthly income would be going to our PITI payment if we had this amount of income. That's great! Low ratios are good news since they signal that only a small amount of your gross monthly income is going for your house payment.

But what if your ratio is higher than the standard 28 percent on conventional loans? What can you do? Although we cover this in detail in Step #8, here are some preliminary ideas.

 A high ratio indicates that you're trying to buy a champagne-budget house on a beer-budget income. The options are to shop for a lower-priced house, find a larger down payment, go with a house that has lower property taxes (to get your payment down), or find a loan that would allow a higher ratio, such as a Federal Housing Administration (FHA)-insured loan.

As soon as you uncover your credit, you'll be ready to contact a lender to do a professional analysis of your loan capabilities. Once your analysis of the qualification form is complete, IT'S YOUR MOVE ✦

Uncover and Understand Your Credit Picture

Whoever said "what you don't know won't hurt you" obviously never checked his credit! Of all the potential roadblocks in the housebuying process, poor credit can prove to be one of the most difficult ones to overcome.

The strongest approach is to look at your credit report *before* starting the home search and well in advance of a loan application (two to four months is advised). This will alert you to who has reported what about your credit history and can point out errors that need correcting.

Early review of your credit picture is particularly important if you have been previously married and have not checked the report since the divorce. Credit postings (particularly negative ones) of a former spouse have a habit of haunting the previous joint report and are usually not adequately addressed before the divorce gavel raps. This means that obligations must be sorted out on both former spouses' credit reports, creditors notified of the changes, and perhaps even a new qualifying process completed for the party assuming sole responsibility for a debt.

Accessing your credit can, as I say, let you know what everybody else already knows about you! Let's cover the steps you need to take.

Step 1. Access Your Credit Report

To uncover credit information on yourself, you need to know how the system works.

The credit reporting system nationwide consists of three major reporting agencies: TRW, Equifax, and Trans Union. (See Figure 3.5 with names and numbers of their central locations.) For less than $20, you can receive your credit report from one of the three national credit reporting bureaus. (If you've been denied credit, employment, or insurance because of credit in the past 60 days, the report is free.)

While all three agencies are independent companies, they have the ability to merge their information. When you first order your report, ask if you can receive a merged report; if not, it's good to purchase all three reports so you receive the complete picture. It's a small price to pay for peace of mind.

Here's how to get a copy of your consumer report:

1. Check the Yellow Pages in your phone book under the heading Credit Reporting Agencies for the company nearest you.
2. Visit the company during its consumer credit hours and request a copy of your report.

FIGURE 3.5   Credit Reporting Bureaus

TRW National Consumer Assistance
P.O. Box 949
Allen, TX 75002
1-800-682-7654

Trans Union Credit Corporation
P.O. Box 390
Springfield, PA 19064
1-800-851-2674

EQUIFAX SERVICES
P.O. Box 740193
Atlanta, GA 30374
1-800-685-1111

You must provide the following:
- A picture i.d.
- Your full name
- Social Security number
- Date of birth
- Current address
- Any previous addresses for the past five years (including ZIP codes)
- Name of your employer
- Telephone number
- The same information for your spouse (if applicable)
- Your signature and the date of your request (spouse must also sign if a joint request)
- The processing fee (if applicable)
3. If you call the nationwide numbers (see Figure 3.5) to order your report, you must include all information requested on the phone message for the particular reporting agency. For example, TRW requests that in order to protect your privacy, you must provide one of the following: a copy of a photo i.d., such as your driver's license, or a photocopy of a recent billing statement from a major creditor showing your current address, or a copy of a utility billing. (Note: Equifax allows your request to be

charged to a major credit card; TRW will send you one annual complimentary copy of your own report.)

4. If you apply in person, you will have your report in a matter of minutes. Via mail, it may take seven to ten working days. Either way, you'll receive detailed instructions on how to decipher the many symbols and notations on the report.

The report you'll receive as an individual is called a "consumer report" or "in-file report." Though less in-depth than the mortgage credit report required by lenders, it will give you a good idea of your credit history.

Step 2. Decipher Your Credit Report

Never assume that your credit report is "clean" just because you've been financially responsible. As mentioned previously, items can post to your credit report by accident without your being aware of them.

So what will your credit report tell you? A lot! In addition to the general information regarding your address, Social Security number, date of birth, employer, and spouse's name (if applicable), major categories include the following:

- Your legal relationship to the account. Using a credit agency association code, this portion of your report will show if your account is under one name (individual), joint, or has a comaker/cosigner.
- Account status and history. This section lists all open and paid accounts, the current status of the account, and the last payment received as reported by the creditor, including a past payment history (showing late payments and/or collections). By law, negative credit information can remain on a report for seven years and bankruptcies for ten years. These negative postings are sometimes not removed from the report automatically, and you need to monitor their removal. Good credit stays on a report indefinitely.
- Balance owing and highest amount owed. These two sections are found side by side and tell quite a tale! They will show not only the balance owing as of the creditor's last report, but also what the highest amount owed has been

(which may or may not be your line of credit). For example, ABC credit card company might report that while your current balance is zero, your highest balance was previously maxed out at $10,000 (and it occurred three months after the credit card was issued!). We'll see later how the lender might interpret this type of leverage.

- Public record information. All items of public record affecting the financial obligations of the consumer—bankruptcies, liens, judgments, divorce, child support, *lis pendens* (pending law suits)—are included in this section. Any postings here are important to the lender because they can indicate financial trouble and/or affect the equity position of a lender who makes you a loan.

- Who has made credit inquiries. This section shows who has checked your credit, usually as far back as approximately two years. Most consumers are unaware that *anyone* can check your credit for a valid business reason! In fact, federal credit reporting law states that while the party must have a valid business reason, it is not required that the consumer sign anything authorizing the check, although many creditors do require a signature as a legal precaution.

If you disagree that a valid business reason existed, under federal law you can take the party to court. If found guilty, the perpetrator could be fined up to $5,000 (you get the money!) and could be imprisoned for up to one year. If for no other reason, pulling your credit report will show you who has checked your credit. It's certainly your right to know.

What about too many credit inquiries? Is that okay? It depends. A mortgage lender might be hesitant to make a loan to someone who has had an abundance of credit inquiries in the past six months. This could serve as a red flag to the lender that the party was denied credit, is accumulating open lines of credit to borrow against, or is leveraging assets before declaring bankruptcy. This also applies to individuals checking their own credit reports repeatedly, as though they were waiting for something adverse to be posted. Whatever the reason, the lender may want an explanation.

Step 3. Determine Whether You Have "Good Credit"

Once you've deciphered your credit picture, how can you tell if you have good credit? Fannie Mae (Federal National Mortgage Association) is an investor company that purchases a large share of the mortgage loans generated in the United States. It has set the following guidelines for good credit that many lenders use when underwriting mortgage loans. (Note: The most recent 18-month period has the most bearing on the lender's evaluation.)

- Revolving debt "good credit" (such as credit card obligations): No payments 60 days or more past due; no more than two payments 30 days past due (typically within the past eighteen months). Provide explanations for all late payments.
- Installment debt "good credit" (such as car payments and other installment loans): No payments 60 days or more past due; no more than one payment 30 days past due. Provide explanations for all late payments.
- Housing debt "good credit" (includes mortgages and rent payments): No payments past due! Timely payment can be verified by the borrower's cancelled checks for the last 12 months, loan payment history from the mortgage servicer or credit report reference, or the borrower's year-end mortgage account statement (if it includes payment receipt history).

You may be thinking, "I'll never meet these guidelines—my credit isn't perfect!" Don't fear. While the lender wants to see that the borrower's intent was to have perfect credit, lenders allow for minor glitches along the way. The truth is, things can happen that are outside of human control! The mortgage lender you use may also use a new method of credit evaluation called "credit scoring." This is gaining national prominence as yet another test of the borrower's potential to repay the loan. Done electronically, it allocates certain values to various items of measurement, such as how many open credit accounts the borrower has, the relationship of the borrower's overall debt to income, etc. Although many lenders use it in tandem with the traditional credit report, it's quickly becoming yet another interpretation of how well a borrower might perform on repaying a loan. If you've checked your credit report and have a good idea of what good credit would look like to the lender (even if yours isn't perfect), IT'S YOUR MOVE ➴

**Understand That the Lender *May*
Accept Some Negative Credit**

While each situation is weighed on a case-by-case basis, adverse credit might be justified if caused by the following:

- Death in the family
- Loss of job (especially industrywide layoffs)
- Severe illness (applicant or member of immediate family)
- Divorce
- Other circumstances outside of borrower's control

Lenders are human and they do want to make loans. If you are upfront and honest about the circumstances surrounding your less-than-perfect credit, the lender will be equally honest in doing everything possible to work with the situation to help you get a loan.

It's important to note that sharing this information with the lender when you prequalify is the best bet (since she will see it on the credit report anyway!). Earlier is definitely better when it comes to overcoming potential credit obstacles. If you've analyzed your credit report (the good and the bad), IT'S YOUR MOVE ♠

 **Repair Credit
Report Errors**

When you first review your credit report, you may find errors caused by improperly reported items by creditors or even credit postings that just aren't yours. Freeing these errors from your report may be tedious, but it can be accomplished and is important to do. So let's review the most likely areas where credit errors may appear.

Similar names confused.   If you have a common name like Smith, Brown, or Jones, or are a junior or senior, you are most likely to have someone else's credit on your report. Even though names, Social Security numbers, and addresses are used to report credit, errors still occur. Upon finding someone else's credit on his report, I once heard a man comment, "Well, if it's *good* credit, maybe I'll keep it!" The problem is that an additional account, yours or not, could signal extra debt to the lender, which might not be good news for qualifying!

Multiple entries of the same account. What could be wrong with multiple entries of the same account on your credit report? Perhaps plenty, because the lender makes a decision based on both the amount of current debts carried by the applicant as well as potential credit at his disposal.

Here's an example. If you had duplicate entries of the same credit card showing a $4,000 open line of credit with zero balances, that's $8,000 in potential credit you could tap. In qualifying you for a loan, the lender may consider that there's a minimum payment on both accounts (or $15 if the minimum amount is unknown). This would be considered a long-term debt, adding $30 per month to your long-term debt picture. The rationale is that you could obtain that money at any time, adding more monthly payments that could strain your ability to pay your new mortgage.

How to Correct Errors on Your Credit Report

1. File a consumer dispute form with the reporting agency, stating that you disagree with the report. (A form will usually accompany your credit report.) Be as specific as you can, for example: "This is not my account. This is my uncle's, John V. Smith, of 402 Oak, Riverside, FL 88888."

   By law, the credit reporting agency must investigate the complaint in a timely manner and report back to you (usually in less than 30 days). If the creditor does not substantiate the posting in that time, the bureau must remove the information.

   The key here is to state that you want the credit reporting agency to inform you in writing when the error is corrected and that you will check your report within 30 days to make sure it has been done. (Do recheck your report, but wait 60 days since it takes time to process the change.)

2. Send a copy of the dispute to the creditor as well, pointing out the mistake.

3. If you resolve the dispute to your satisfaction, have the creditor send letters to all three credit bureaus, asking that they change the information. If it has been a creditor error, federal law states that the credit bureau must send out an amended report to anyone who received a copy during the time the error showed on your report.

If you do not reach a satisfactory conclusion with the creditor, you can place up to a 100-word explanation on your credit report telling your side of the story. This posting is valid for six months, but can be renewed indefinitely in six-month increments.

Should you encounter problems with an uncooperative credit reporting agency (which happens very rarely), you could file a complaint with their monitoring entity, the Federal Trade Commission. You can write to them Attn: Correspondence Department, Room 692, Washington, DC 30580.

Troubleshooting Coborrower Debt— a Growing Problem!

If you've been a coborrower on an obligation or have had joint credit in a marriage, it may affect your credit picture when you apply for a loan if you haven't removed your name from those obligations with creditors.

A common situation occurs when someone applies for credit after a divorce, only to find that the car and corresponding payment awarded to the former spouse is still showing as a joint obligation on the loan applicant's credit report. Ideally, amending the situation should have occurred before the gavel rapped at the divorce (when the applicant still had some leverage). But now the lender is concerned that if the former spouse either hasn't made the car payments or could fail to make them in the future, the applicant would be held responsible for paying them.

What can the borrower do? The lender will suggest alternatives, which might include providing a divorce decree that legally divides the assets and proving that the former spouse has made the car payment (usually for the preceding 12-month period). This could be done by providing photocopies of the canceled checks to the lender.

You can visualize how much fun this might be for the applicant to call his former spouse and say, "Since my new wife and I want to buy our dream house, would you please go back through your last 12 bank statements and photocopy all of the canceled car payment checks (front and back) so that we can qualify for our new loan? And we need all this by tomorrow morning. We knew you wouldn't mind helping us!" Not easy or realistic, is it?

What if you can't pull enough clarifying documentation together to satisfy the lender? The last alternative is to *beg!* Try to convince the lender that the loan the former spouse is paying is not delinquent and hopefully will remain current. Second, point out all of your financial strengths to the lender, which should more than aptly compensate for the loan in question. These could include low monthly debt payments, strong assets, and/or good stable income. Try to offset the potential negative with strengths of your own. A lender who wants to make you the loan will try to find a way to sell your situation to the loan underwriter, so give the lender the necessary ammunition.

Don't forget that anyone can have credit history in his or her own name, even married individuals. Should your spouse die or should you divorce, your personal history is intact and you won't have to re-establish what it took you many years to build. The credit reporting agency is able to assemble your own personal file (which will also show your co-obligations with that spouse) in a matter of minutes from the information contained in their database.

If you've repaired errors on your report (or will do so shortly), then IT'S YOUR MOVE ♣

 ## Close Credit Accounts

What about accounts, such as credit cards or lines of credit, that you no longer use or you attempted to close previously but were never removed from the report? Now may be the time to remove them so that they don't count against your qualifying ratios. (Remember, adverse credit postings will remain on the report for seven years so there's no escaping this reality!)

I've found that the following three-step approach works in closing credit accounts:

1. Notify the creditor in writing that you request to close the account. (This next item is very important.) Be sure to note in the letter that you wish the account to reflect the statement "closed at consumer's request." This way, it won't appear that the creditor closed the account on you! Also, state in the letter that you will be checking your credit report in 30 days to make sure that the account has been closed. (This alerts the creditor that you mean business!)

2. If you want to make sure the creditor receives your letter, you can send the request by certified mail with a return receipt. If you still have a credit card, cut it up (so it can't be intercepted in the mail and used) and send it along. It's a good idea to tape the credit card pieces to the letter you send the creditor and take a photocopy of it for your records before you mail it.

3. Do check your credit report again to make sure the errors have been removed. But it's wise to wait 60 days (instead of 30) to allow time for the information to cycle through the credit system.

One last note on closing accounts. Since you are checking your credit at this point to get a preview of what the lender will see later, you may not want to close out accounts until you formally meet with the lender. You could be making a financial misstep by closing an account that could be an asset to your closing the loan (e.g., a line of credit that could assist you in finding additional monies for closing costs).

Removing Your Name from Marketing Lists

After you've corrected errors and closed accounts on your credit report, you may want to do one last thing: ask to have your name removed from direct mail marketing lists. If you find yourself plagued with tons of junk mail, it may be just what the doctor ordered!

Many creditors do sell our names on mailing lists to other companies. But as a consumer, you have a right to remove your name from those lists using one of two methods.

First, you can contact any of the credit reporting agencies and fill out a form with them. They will make sure it gets into the central direct mail list system.

Or you can go directly to the source, the Direct Marketing Association. Send your written request to Attn: Mail Preference Service, P.O. Box 9008, Farmingdale, NY 11735.

Be sure to evaluate the pros and cons of removing your name. Not only will the solicitations cease (or at least dwindle), the benefits of low-interest-rate credit offers, catalogs, and free subscriptions will dry up as well. The credit reporting agency can give you a good idea of what to expect if you do take this action.

If you've needed to close out unused accounts and have done so, IT'S YOUR MOVE ✦

Repair Damaged Credit

We mentioned earlier in this Step the types of blemished credit the lender might accept when making a loan, including circumstances of illness, job loss, and divorce. But what if you weren't quite as vigilant as you should have been in controlling your credit and now need damage control? What steps can you take to rebuild your credit?

First, don't assume that adverse credit will kill the loan until you get feedback from the lender. Credit problems vary in degree of severity, and yours may not be as severe as they seem.

Second, do all you can to show your intention to improve your credit. This means managing small credit card balances (or paying them off on a monthly basis), meeting payment deadlines (or paying in advance), and developing a strong pattern of saving each month. The key is to show the lender that previous problems are not likely to happen again and that you are doing everything you can to manage your finances prudently.

If your credit situation is so severe that the lender suggests you seek outside help to untangle it, the Consumer Credit Counseling Service, a nonprofit organization with locations throughout the United States, may be one alternative.

This organization evaluates your income, your ability to pay, and your debt load and requests that you surrender your monthly income to them for paying your creditors. The idea is to make things manageable for you until you can get back on your feet. The address for the office nearest you can be found by looking under Credit in the Yellow Pages of your phone book.

Before taking this or any approach where your funds are managed by someone else, be sure to ask the lender if using this system of debt management will be seen as a positive or a negative once you are ready to qualify for a loan.

It's possible that your damaged credit has been caused by a previous bankruptcy. If you need to address this issue, then IT'S YOUR MOVE ♦

 ## Work Around a Previous Bankruptcy

Bankruptcy doesn't have to signal that you can never get a mortgage loan to own your own home; it just takes a little more work.

What will most lenders require before they will make a loan to a party who has declared bankruptcy?

1. The borrower must have re-established credit and have all obligations current. Depending on the lender and the type of loan sought, most lenders will require that two years pass since the discharge of the bankruptcy before making a home loan. While there can be exceptions, this is considered a sound rule of thumb.

2. The borrower must also explain *why* the bankruptcy occurred. A full written description and supporting documentation will be required.

3. Finally, the lender needs to be fairly convinced that bankruptcy would be unlikely to happen again. What has happened to change the circumstances and put you back on the right track? This is important to the lender and can be proven to the degree that you have re-established yourself financially.

The opposite of bankruptcy—having established no credit at all—could pose a roadblock when applying for a mortgage. If you need assistance here, then IT'S YOUR MOVE ♦

 **Establish Credit If You Have None**

What if, instead of adverse credit, you have no credit? Some potential homebuyers see the only alternative as racing out to apply for multiple credit cards. Based on what we've covered previously, this may not be the best tactic. Remember that even if you have zero balances on credit cards, the lender may consider that they have minimum repayments for the purpose of qualifying. For marginally qualified buyers, this could drive qualifying ratios sky high!

Sound ways to establish credit might include the following:

1. Use the down payment you have to collateralize an installment loan of 60, 90, or 120 days (the longer the better if you have the time to wait before your purchase). If possible, take out the loan with the lender you'll use for the mortgage. Your prompt repayments will help you establish a good credit reference, one you can use for your loan application.

2. Document your use of cash to pay obligations. This can be done by obtaining credit letters of reference from utility companies, small retailers, or anywhere your good payment records show you've paid cash.

3. If you know your overall debt is low and you won't jeopardize your qualifying by doing it, apply for one credit card (bank cards like Mastercard or Visa are good bets). The key here is not to run up high debt, and pay the balance in full each month. (Again, you're best off doing this only after you have been preliminarily prequalified with a lender.)

4. Remember the statement we used to open this chapter: "Prepare in advance of need." If you know that a home purchase is somewhere in your future, establish good credit now and monitor it for accuracy. It will go a long way in helping you get that loan.

If you've looked in your wallet and have tackled the 11 corresponding challenges, congratulations, IT'S YOUR MOVE to Homebuying Step #4 ↘

If you fail to meet the 11 CHALLENGE CARD requirements of "Look in Your Wallet," GO TO THE PENALTY BOX.

Penalty Box

Possible penalties for failing to check out your finances include the following:

1. Trying to purchase (and losing) a house you love because you failed to complete the How Much Can You Afford? worksheet and had no idea what you could qualify for
2. Being unable to buy a home until your credit picture is repaired and errors removed
3. Jumping ahead in the homebuying sequence (naughty, naughty—remember our promise!) and finding that your offers are not accepted by sellers since your financial picture (assets and debts) are not in place

For "help" out of the PENALTY BOX:

1. Vow again that you'll only tackle the homebuying steps in the proper sequence. Tackling them out of order will get you into deeper trouble!
2. Use the checklists provided to pull all of your asset and debt information together (this will help for our visit to the lender in Step #4).
3. Pull a copy of your credit report and make sure it's free of errors (and other people's credit postings!).

 Take Trump Card #3

If you're diligent in sorting out and pulling together the financial information we've cited in this Step (including troubleshooting your credit report), you'll "wow" the lender, speed through the loan process, and be ordering the moving van!

Step
4

Let the Lender Look in Your Wallet

I'm proud of you—you've taken the time to pull together information about your assets and debts, and you've even checked your credit report. And because you know what everybody else already knew about your credit (or they could find out if they had a valid business reason), it's time to let the lender look in your wallet!

Formal prequalifying with the lender *before* househunting very rarely happened in the past. Based on what we have covered previously about homebuying emotions, credit gliches, and heavy debt, it's amazing that as many sales closed as did!

The order of events in today's homebuying process is quite different. If you want to be a successful homebuyer, you'll tackle the steps in the most logical and financially safe order. After fully investigating your own finances, you'll contact the lender to prequalify, then proceed to find the agent and/or the property.

Five Reasons to Talk Financing First!

You can be prequalified for a loan in various ways, but meeting with the financing source before doing anything else is potentially the most reliable way. Here's why.

1. You will know exactly what you can afford and how much cash will be required to make that purchase. If you need to gather more cash for closing or find a gift letter to help out with the down payment, you'll have time to do it.
2. Any credit gliches that might stall the loan process can hopefully be addressed upon first contact with the lender.
3. The loan you can qualify for will match the property you select. Not all property may be approved for certain types of financing if it can't meet the specified physical requirements. In addition, sellers may not want to pay the costs involved (such as points) to help you secure a certain type of financing.
4. You can enter the active buyer market in a much stronger position. If you are prequalified or preapproved (as we'll cover later), you will have a definite advantage in getting your offer accepted by a seller. Additionally, you can concentrate solely on selecting the best property instead of worrying about the loan to come. And if you find your dream home, you can feel confident making a full-price offer to secure the property, knowing that the financing is there.
5. Based on the type of financing you choose, you can structure your offer to address the appropriate costs, closing time, and advantages of that loan. This will show the seller that you are a serious buyer who has done your homework, and it will do much to eliminate surprises in the sale.

Choose *Your* Most Comfortable Way to Visit with the Lender

Even though the end result is the same, with today's technology you may have your first contact with a lender in person, over the phone, through electronic mail (e-mail), or even over the Internet.

As a motivated buyer, you may find it most convenient to prequalify with the lender over the phone. In a matter of a few minutes, the lender will pull your credit report, do a thumbnail sketch of your debts and assets, and have a pretty good idea of your qualifying ability. Currently, some lenders in the United States take the formal application over the phone and then send paperwork by hard copy (either fax or mail) for the borrower to sign. Or, as in Step #4, the lender may take applications online over the Internet. In the future, it's totally possible that the borrower may never meet the lender face-to-face.

As was stated previously, the lender needs only a valid business reason to check your credit—with or without your written approval (although most lenders make it a point to get a written authorization signed by you before they check your credit). Keep in mind that a number of credit inquiries by lenders could be a concern if you're shopping for interest rates and points over the phone with various companies, because your credit may be checked by each lender in turn. This is not necessarily a problem, but once you decide to make formal application with a particular lender, you may have to explain other credit inquiries by competing firms! The lender needs to make sure that you are not getting loans from other lenders simultaneously or that you were turned down by other companies.

Some lenders today are not only using computers to input data, but also to help them make lending decisions. Computer programs can use AI (artificial intelligence) to compare an applicant's capacity to buy with computer models of characteristics found in other successful loan candidates. Applicants who fail to fit the guidelines are then referred to a real person, who will evaluate the loan on an individual basis. Lenders feel this process is also beneficial to make lending less discriminatory.

If you're convinced that talking financing to the lender is definitely in your best interests, then IT'S YOUR MOVE ✎

 ## Choose the *Lender* You're Most Comfortable With

It stands to reason that if you're going to be baring your finances (and everything else but your birthmark) to someone, you had better be able to like, trust, and communicate well with that lender. So how do you go about choosing a lender?

First, it makes sense to give repeat business to someone you've worked well with before. In fact, you may be able to negotiate a better rate and fees by doing so. (Don't forget this when looking for refinancing money as well, because the lender holding your existing loan usually doesn't want to lose your business.)

Second, ask around—query both real estate agents and friends. Most real estate agents have a good idea of who gives the quickest processing and best rates, but consumers are the best benchmark of quality service. Questions to ask others who have previously used lenders you're considering include the following: Did the lender explain the loan process well? Was the lender competitive in rates and fees as well as fair? Did the lender communicate well with you or were there breakdowns? Why would or wouldn't they do another loan with that lender?

Instead of being referred to a real person, you may hear a company endorsed instead. And it's no longer only the traditional bank on the corner or the good old savings and loan downtown that's competing. Mortgage companies (also called mortgage bankers) are a solid and very competitive source of loans. They originate loans and sell them to investors after closing. Because many mortgage companies do business nationwide, they may be a viable source of funds for your mortgage, especially if you live in a "geographically challenged" location where there are few (if any) lenders.

Or you might be interested in working with a mortgage broker, who will scout out loans that match your needs and then collect a fee (from the loan) for doing so. If you're less than a grade A credit risk, mortgage brokers can shop for B grade, or even higher-risk lenders who may take your loan. And because most mortgage brokers are paid only on the loans that close, they are motivated to provide quick turnaround times for borrowers.

Don't overlook credit unions in your area. They have blossomed as mortgage sources, especially for second mortgages and equity lines, and may offer fairly competitive interest rates and very low processing charges.

One last point about choosing a lender. Always keep in mind any other upcoming financing you may need, such as for a car loan. You might be able to entice a lender to give you a very competitive rate on your mortgage if he/she knew there would be other business to follow (based on the type of loans available with that lender).

Now that you've selected the lender you're most comfortable with, IT'S YOUR MOVE ♣

 ## Know If You'll Be Prequalified or Preapproved

If you purchased a home more than five years ago and visited the lender before you chose the property, chances are you were *prequalified*. But today, a variation on that theme might find you *preapproved* before you find the property.

What *is* the difference? Think of preapproval as a higher level of prequalifying. With prequalifying, your credit is checked and the lender tells you how much house payment you can qualify for. But with preapproval, you not only have a thumbnail sketch of what you can afford, but you are given approval that you will get the loan you need in a specified amount provided nothing changes in your financial picture. It's like being a cash buyer!

This deeper level of approval comes from providing the lender with more documentation. Although the requirements can vary from lender to lender, most will minimally require your last three pay stubs (preferably showing your year-to-date salary), a copy of your checking and savings account statements for the past three months, and a mortgage credit report that the lender will access.

Some preapprovals are contingent upon receiving an acceptable appraisal on the property; others are not. But you can see how being preapproved for a loan can elevate your position in the eyes of the seller, who will know that you're "good for the money."

In lieu of being prequalified or preapproved with the lender (or in addition to), you may choose to take the next route. If so, IT'S YOUR MOVE ♣

 ## Understand the Degree to Which a Real Estate Agent Can Qualify You

It's perfectly fine to have a real estate professional such as an agent or a builder prequalify you, but with two conditions: (1) They are knowledgeable and feel comfortable doing it; and

(2) you feel comfortable letting them! Most real estate agents will do at least a thumbnail version of qualifying before showing property. This keeps them from showing you properties you can't afford and also helps them test your motivation and your financial capacity to purchase.

But in most cases, the prequalifying that a real estate agent or builder does is merely a precursor to what the lender will do.

In the past several years, more agents suggest that buyers be prequalifed or preapproved with lenders before the househunting begins. This makes the buyer's negotiating position stronger and helps the agent structure the offer, noting the type of financing and costs that will need to be shared by the parties.

In today's full-service real estate environment, you may work with a real estate company that has the capacity to be both agent and lender. Some brokers are adding mortgage divisions to their companies, either with separate loan originators on staff or with agents serving as both property salespersons and loan originators.

Through computerized loan origination (CLO) systems, brokers can have access to a selection of mortgage brokers via a computer database. Each lender has a variety of loan programs that can be shopped by the agent and buyer. Not only does the CLO add loan fee income to the broker's business, but real estate agents who work under this system report that they like the "full service" approach that originating the loan and controlling the sale affords.

Once a loan program is selected, the borrower's financial information and formal application are sent electronically to the mortgage broker, who then processes the loan.

When the mortgage is ready to close, the loan documents are sent electronically to the agent for closing the sale. Just as we saw previously with lenders, this approach (combined with others in the financing chapter) can futuristically cut precious days off your loan closing.

IT'S YOUR MOVE

Sail Smoothly through the Loan Application Interview

For some buyers, the loan interview is the most nail-biting part of homebuying. They worry about what the lender will ask, whether they'll have the right answers, and, mostly, if they'll qualify for the loan they need.

The best way to cut down on stress is to follow the Boy Scout motto: Be prepared! Information is definitely power when it comes to making a loan application, so let's cover the questions the lender will ask so you'll know what to expect.

If the lender hasn't done so already (such as during a phone call), she will pull a credit report on you and any coborrower. A more in-depth report than what you saw on yourself, this is called a mortgage credit report; it shows a deeper analysis of your credit, including a merged report from two of the three credit reporting agencies. This report will form the foundation for your formal loan application to come.

What the Lender Will Ask You to Provide

Here's where all the financial information you've pulled together on yourself comes in. The lender will ask you about your annual income and what debts you owe, as well as any other source of income (such as child support, alimony, or separate maintenance income).

The following is an in-depth look at the information the lender will ask you to provide:

1. Property Information
   - A copy of the purchase agreement; a copy of the listing agreement (if available); for new construction, a copy of plans and specifications; if other than single-family residential, information about the property including number of units and year built
   - Legal description of the property
   - Any other property information available including plat map, zoning information, etc.
2. Borrower Information
   - Full names, Social Security numbers, and ages of all loan applicants and/or coborrowers

- Residence addresses for the past two years
- Names and addresses of employers for the last two years (Give address for the personnel office, since this may be different from the physical address of the company.)

3. Asset Information

- Income: W-2 forms and perhaps federal income tax returns from the past two years. General qualifying requirements: A two-year work history in the same line of work with an explanation of any employment gaps (Be sure to include information about time spent in formal education or career training, because this may count toward the two-year employment criterion. Raises guaranteed to begin within 60 days of loan closing can be counted as qualifying income. Part-time income requires a two-year track record and strong probability that the work will continue.)
- Two most recent paycheck stubs
- Two most recent bank statements
- Checking account numbers and locations
- Savings account numbers and locations
- IRA/Keogh account information and locations
- Credit union account numbers and locations
- Stocks and bonds (company name and description)
- Life insurance net cash value
- Market value of real estate owned
- Net worth of businesses owned
- Automobiles owned (make and year)
- Other income: The following describes how the lender will treat other types of income. (Note that income such as child support and alimony need not be included if you do not want it to be considered for loan qualifying.)

Child support: Proof of receipts are required through a printout from the court or 12 months of canceled checks. Payments must have been received on time for at least 12 months and be scheduled to continue at minimum another 36 months to count as qualifying income, depending on the loan program.

Social Security income and disability payments: The buyer must provide a copy of the award letter and a recent check stub or copy of a bank statement if deposited by direct deposit.

Pension income: The buyer should provide a check stub and any forms showing the duration of payments.

Rental property income: Verify by providing income tax returns and schedules from the past two years. Only 75 percent of the rental income is counted, but 100 percent of the expenses are debts. Leases also should be provided to the lender.

Overtime: Depending on the type of loan, lenders will look for a two-year history and consider your average amount of overtime will continue (unless your employer says something to the contrary). If the overtime can't be verified, it might still be considered as a "compensating factor," but it will not count towards qualifying income.

A bonus can be considered (usually averaged) if the applicant has received it for the past two years.

Other receivables include a gift letter or explanation of the source of funds for the down payment and/or closing costs or documentation for any other monies owed you.

4. Debt Information
   - Mortgages/home equity loans: Documentation of current mortgages/equity loans as well as recently paid off mortgages
   - If renting a home, a copy of current lease
   - Payment books or monthly billing statements for debts you owe
   - Information on car loans (Timely repayments of larger loans like this are good verification that you do take your obligations seriously.)
   - Information about outstanding student loans
   - Information about any payments made as a direct withdrawal from a checking account or a credit union
   - Letter(s) of explanation for any late payments, judgments, liens, or previous foreclosures
   - A copy of any previous bankruptcy proceedings with current status and full explanation of why the bankruptcy occurred
   - Information about any other debt you've paid off that could serve as a good reference

5. How the Lender and Underwriter View Debt

The secondary market considers long-term debt used for qualifying to be any debt that can't be paid off in ten months (or is recurring). Note: Local lenders can choose to be more restrictive and can err on the side of caution (i.e., stating that long-term debt is that which extends more than *six* months). Lenders also have the right to consider any "substantial" debt as part of the long-term debt picture. For example, a car payment of $450 with five payments remaining might be seen as significant enough in a marginal borrower to put stress on repaying the mortgage loan.

6. Other Debt Concerns
   - Previous bankruptcies—the underwriter generally requires that the bankruptcy be discharged (and credit satisfactorily re-established) for a period of 24 months before loan application. (Exceptions can be made, especially if the lender can be shown that the bankruptcy occurred through extenuating circumstances outside the borrower's control.)
   - Previous foreclosure. This is the toughest of underwriting hurdles. The lender would need to show why the foreclosure occurred and that it is unlikely to occur again (e.g., caused by death or illness in the family, divorce, etc.).

7. Other Information That May Be Required
   - A copy of any divorce decree or separate maintenance agreement to document alimony and/or child support
   - If a VA loan, Certificate of Eligibility and DD214
   - If applicant is a nonresident, copy of Certificate of Resident Alien Status ("green card")
   - A check for the credit report, appraisal, and any application fee

8. If You're Self-Employed (categorized as having 25 percent or more interest in a business that employs you)
   - You need the items previously stated plus: two years of signed copies of complete income tax returns (with schedules attached)
   - A balance sheet for the previous two years (audited or prepared by an accountant or professional tax preparer)
   - If you are a sole proprietor, a profit and loss statement

- If the business is a corporation, an S corporation, or a partnership, signed copies of the past two years of federal business-income tax returns (with schedules attached), a year-to-date profit and loss statement, and a business credit report
- If you work on full commission, W-2s and signed tax returns for the past two years plus a year-to-date income statement. Income is typically averaged over the time period reported and should show signs of either being stable or increasing—not declining.
- Note: The self-employed applicant must provide extensive documentation to the lender. This is generally a mandate from the secondary market (where loans are purchased), because there is greater room for a self-employed borrower to embellish verifications—the applicant is both the employee and the employer! We cover exceptions to these underwriting guidelines (low-doc/no-doc loans and portfolio lending) later in this Step.

What the Lender Will Ask You

The lender will ask you questions from the loan application (also known as the standard Freddie Mac/Fannie Mae application) and review the documents you've brought to the appointment. Once she crunches the numbers (either on her financial calculator or on a laptop computer), she'll determine your qualifying ratios and how much house you can afford. This will take into consideration your approximate down payment, the money you have for closing costs, and the maximum interest rate you can handle.

The lender's job is to compile information that can be passed on to the loan underwriter to approve your loan. (We'll cover the underwriting process in a minute.) So it's in your best interest to answer questions as completely as possible. This is not the time to have "selective memory," particularly about debts you owe. The conduits of information the lender will access during the loan process are more than likely to uncover the information. And by signing the loan application, you state that you have told the truth to the best of your knowledge. To do otherwise is to commit perjury, which is punishable by fine, imprisonment, or both under

Title 18 of the United States Code. Pretty stiff potential penalties for a little "lapse of memory"!

The lender won't be asking you any question that would discriminate against you or is founded on race, color, sex, creed, or national origin. An example of how things have changed is that back in the 1950s, women were asked if they planned on having a family under the assumption that they would then leave the work force, leaving only one income to pay the loan. Thank heavens, times have changed!

What You Will Be Asked to Sign

You'll be asked to sign a variety of papers, including verifications of employment (that the lender sends to your employer), verifications of deposit (that the lender sends to verify funds on deposit), and the loan application.

On the application, you'll also be asked to state your race, nation of origin, and sex under the section entitled "Information for Government Monitoring Purposes." This can be confusing if not explained correctly by the lender, since it could appear to be a form of discrimination. The contrary is true. This information monitors the lender's compliance with the Equal Credit Opportunity Act, fair housing laws, and home mortgage disclosure laws. It also monitors the number and types of minorities being afforded the opportunity to apply for a home loan. And because the information becomes part of a national database to help monitor and reduce discrimination, it's advised that you answer the questions.

While it is not mandatory that you answer these questions, if you decline, the lender is required by law to complete the questions himself based on your appearance and/or your surnames.

What the Lender Will Give You

Either at the loan application interview or up to three days after, the lender is required by law to provide the borrower with several sets of information. These include the costs incurred with the loan, the effective interest rate being charged, and the possibility that the lender will be transferring the loan servicing rights or "selling the loan" after closing.

The Real Estate Settlement Procedures Act (RESPA) requires disclosure of estimated settlement costs that you'll pay. It is itemized on a detailed statement that includes fees to be paid at closing. Note: These are merely good faith estimates based on the time of application and can vary slightly based on changes that occur between the application and closing dates. Additionally, the lender is required to provide you with HUD's *Settlement Cost Guide* booklet describing the homebuying process.

The purpose of the federal Truth-in-Lending Act is to help you understand the terms of credit being extended to you as well as the cost of that credit. This helps you compare loan programs and lenders.

For example, the lender must disclose the annual percentage rate (APR) to you expressed as a yearly rate. It adds the points, fees, and insurance costs on top of the interest rate—that's why the APR you see on the disclosure form will be higher than the note rate interest you're paying in your payment.

In general, the APR is a good way to compare two loans for cost-effectiveness. But there is a catch. Lenders have some latitude about including various loan fees in the APR. While the Truth-in-Lending Act requires that refundable fees (those you would get back if you didn't qualify) must be included in the APR, nonrefundable fees do not have to be factored into the APR. Thus, two identical loans with two different lenders could have different APRs! This is confusing at best when you're trying to decide which loan will cost you less.

You can ask potential lenders which fees they are including in the APR calculation and keep that in mind when comparing loans. Most borrowers will, instead, focus solely on comparing the rate, points, fees, and insurance payments. Since these are the major cost components, they're probably a pretty good barometer.

The last disclosure the lender will provide for you at the time of application has to do with the probability that the lender will sell the servicing rights on your loan after it's closed. This practice is called "selling the loan" and the disclosure will tell you what percentage of loans they made in the past were eventually sold to another servicer. (We'll cover your rights when your loan is sold in Step #10.)

If you're considering an adjustable rate mortgage (ARM), the lender will also provide you with an example of how ARMs like the one you're considering have performed in the past. In addition, ask the lender to do a worst-case scenario of the maximum interest rate adjustment over the life of the loan. Ask to see the actual monthly payment amounts, not just the interest rates, since most homebuyers can relate better to payment amounts than to interest rates.

 ## Pose Your Own Questions to the Lender

Before you waste your time with a lender who won't be able to do the job (yes, as found in all other professions, there are some people like that in lending!), you need to interview the lender to get answers to *your* questions. That's right, as the lender asks you questions, you ask your own. Not only will this give you information on the types of loan products the lender provides, but it will give you a hint whether you should work with this lender.

    A competent, professional lender will welcome your questions because he/she has nothing to hide and realizes that if you have the information you need, it will generally make you a better loan applicant.

    Take time to write down your questions before the loan interview. In the excitement of the moment, you may gloss over some of the questions and/or forget to ask them entirely. And if you expect to get answers to make an informed decision about the lender and type of loan that best suits your needs, asking these questions will be crucial.

Ask questions such as the following:

1. Will I be prequalified or preapproved? If preapproved, is there any contingency, such as receiving an acceptable appraisal?
2. Can I have loan comparison sheets for the loans I'm considering, including closing cost comparisons?
3. What about locking in interest rates and points on the loan? For how long is the lock good, and is it a reasonable time period based on when my loan is expected to close? Is there a fee involved for locking in? Is there a provision for unlocking the lock should the rate fall?

4. Does my loan require *private mortgage insurance* (PMI)? If so, which insurers do you use and are their rates competitive? What are their current guidelines for removing the PMI? (While these may not be in effect when you're ready to remove the PMI, it will give you a good indication of what to expect.) If the lender says, "I don't know" or "Don't worry about it," *worry about it* (and also whether or not you should stay with this lender)! We'll cover private mortgage insurance in greater depth in Step #8.
5. Will my monthly payment include taxes and insurance, or could I pay those separately myself? (While this is not always possible based on the type of loan and the lender, if it *is* possible, it makes good business sense to accumulate the funds yourself, including interest!)
6. Since I'm considering loan programs offered by several lenders, what loan terms and concessions are you willing to make in order to write this loan? These could include creativity with points, origination fees, warehousing fees, underwriting fees, and "garbage" (miscellaneous) fees.
7. If you're interested in an adjustable rate mortgage, ask: Will you provide me with a computer printout of the progressions showing how my payment could adjust under a worst-case scenario? (This is a good visual to prepare you for where and when your payment could increase.)
8. How often will you communicate with me? Can I expect a call every week? Good lenders today tell consumers what they can expect in the loan process and when they can expect progress updates. If your lender doesn't volunteer this information, tell her a day of the week and time that's convenient for you to receive a call and intimate that you'll expect it to occur!

If the Lender Fails to Answer Your Questions

A good lender will *not* sidestep questions on purpose. Although she may need to research the question and get back to you, a good lender *will* get back to you in a timely fashion. In the meantime, realize that waiting for answers is usually not costing you money, it's *saving* you some, because you aren't taking an action that could prove a misstep.

 ## Understanding Underwriting

After the lender has gathered information from you and you've decided that you want to work with her, the process of underwriting the loan begins. Underwriting is pulling together your verifications of employment and banking information, reviewing your credit and debts, and deciding if it appears that you can financially handle the mortgage for which you're applying. Based generally on the underwriting guidelines of FNMA (called Fannie Mae), FHLMC (known as Freddie Mac), and GNMA (known as Ginnie Mae)—all of which are purchasers of loans in the secondary market—the underwriter makes a decision of loan approval and communicates it to the lender.

Underwriting can be done by a person on the lender's staff or by a separate underwriting company. Perhaps one of the most misunderstood players in the mortgage process, the underwriter (just like the lender) *really wants* to find a way to approve your loan. (That's why it's important to provide additional information when it's asked of you.)

Providing More Information for the Underwriter

In some cases the underwriter needs more information or clarification of information provided him. So don't be concerned if you're asked to provide additional information. It just means that the underwriter is still piecing the puzzle together, trying to get to a "yes" on your loan.

The most common areas needing clarification and additional information are the following:

1. Gift letters: If all or part of your down payment and/or closing costs are coming from a relative or employer gift, both you and the giver of the funds may be asked additional questions. These questions are not meant to pry; the lender is trying to determine if any of the gifted funds were borrowed by the giver and to attest that the funds did come from legal sources.

2. Divorce decrees: The last thing a divorced person wants is to relive the terms and conditions of a long-settled divorce decree. But clarification, especially as it relates to

the debts of the parties, is often necessary to obtain loan approval.

3. Child support documentation: While court orders and records are the best source of information and proof of payment, alternative documentation may be accepted— but it may take some effort on your part as a loan applicant.

4. IRS liens or other credit gliches: You would assume that if a lien (or other credit glitch) had been satisfied, it would automatically come off your credit report and no longer be an issue. Wrong. Proving that the lien has been satisfied is merely the beginning. Release by the creditor may be required, and rest assured, it won't be verified overnight. (This is yet another reason to check your credit as soon as possible so that you can begin the troubleshooting process to remove satisfied items like this.)

We've covered general loan requirements; but in Step #8, you'll see how they apply to special loan programs.

If you've met the six challenges of "Let the Lender Look in Your Wallet," then congratulations! IT'S YOUR MOVE to Home-buying Step #5   ✦

But if you've fallen short on any of the challenges, GO TO THE PENALTY BOX.

Penalty Box

Possible penalties include the following:

1. Making an offer on a house you can't afford, only to lose it (and your deposit) when you don't qualify
2. Delaying your loan preapproval to stop and gather information on your assets, debts, and income that you should have gathered before visiting the lender
3. Being prevented from buying when you uncover blemishes on your credit report that you should have repaired before visiting the lender
4. Having your offer rejected because the seller wants offers only from buyers who are preapproved or prequalified
5. Paying a hefty fine and serving time in jail for lying about your financial picture to the lender (Yes, it is remote, but makes you stop and think, doesn't it?)

For "help" out of the PENALTY BOX:

1. Assemble your financial information before visiting the lender.
2. Make sure you understand how much house you can afford, whether you are prequalified or preapproved, and feel comfortable working with the lender you've selected. Make sure that the lender is more than willing to answer any questions you have and provide written materials to back up the information.
3. Remind yourself that househunting comes *after* looking in your wallet and visiting the lender—not before!

 Take Trump Card #4

Be proactive when looking for and selecting a lender for your mortgage. The loan process will be much less stressful and more enjoyable if you work with a lender you're comfortable with and can rely on to provide you with the answers you need.

Step
5

Find the Help You Need

If you've just turned to this chapter and have not read the previous four Steps, STOP—DO NOT PASS GO! You could be in big trouble if you proceed before covering the first four Steps in the game!

The rationale is that finding the agent and/or the property before setting the stage with your emotions, timing, and finances could spell disaster. (At least *review* the previous Steps to make sure you can sail through the challenges posed.)

 ## Decide to Go It Alone or Use an Agent

The first challenge in this move is to decide whether you can go it alone, or want/need to get help finding a home. The key to making the right decision lies in part in your buying personality.

Just as in department store shopping, some buyers want the salesperson to lead them to the product, demonstrate it, and point out selection alternatives, while other buyers want to walk into the store and be left alone.

Remember the fairy tale of Red Riding Hood and the wolf? Red Riding Hood was not only the helpful one taking goodies to Grandma, but she also required a lot of information in her quest (albeit it from the wrong source, the wolf!).

The wolf, on the other hand, was on his own mission, needing neither assistance nor input from anyone. He just wanted to get the deed done—by himself!

Two different personalities, two different agendas.

Here are a series of concerns to help determine your buying personality as a Red Riding Hood or a Lone Wolf househunter:

Traits of a Red Riding Hood Househunter

- Somewhat naive about real estate and/or business in general
- A first-time purchaser who has never been through the homebuying process and/or needs help completing the purchase agreement, or a repeat buyer who appreciates letting someone else bring the sale to a close so you can just move in
- More comfortable if a third-party professional gathers information and outlines options regarding neighborhoods, financing, home inspections, and other matters
- Aware that you are best served not negotiating in your own behalf
- Not willing to take the necessary time and effort to tackle the sale alone—more of a team player

Traits of a Lone Wolf Househunter

- Savvy about real estate or business in general
- Knowledgeable about how a real estate sale fits together, including the components of the purchase agreement, earnest money deposits, and the loan process
- A good negotiator (or at least thinks so)
- Focused on househunting in one specific geographic area or subdivision, and knowledgeable about the market values of

those properties, especially the prices of the ones that have sold recently

- Capable of gathering information and processing it without help
- Willing to invest the time it takes to troubleshoot the sale and bring it to closing (including coordinating activities with inspectors, repair persons, appraisers, etc.)
- Doesn't need and/or doesn't appreciate someone else's suggestions on what to do

Notice I didn't say that the wolf is a Big Bad Wolf—there's nothing wrong with finding a house on your own. Just make sure that you fit the profile described and are willing to make the necessary sacrifices in time, effort, and perhaps money. (Yes, it *is* often difficult to negotiate *for* yourself, *by* yourself, as we'll see in Step #7 on negotiating.)

If you're more of a Red Riding Hood buyer, working with a real estate agent and/or other professionals may be more to your liking. But just as Red found when she traveled down that treacherous path to Grandma's, you've got to be able to evaluate the source of the information and its context, and weed out the good advice from the bad.

Once you've decided if accompanied or unaccompanied is for you, IT'S YOUR MOVE 🔖

 ## Find the Right Real Estate Professional to Fit Your Needs

After being involved in real estate for over 20 years as a broker and educator, I'm convinced that matching your *buying personality* to the *selling personality* of the agent is paramount to the success of the transaction and your happiness with the agent.

Here's an illustration. As a salesperson, I tend to be very motivational. Although well structured and methodical, I love to work with buyers who (in addition to being financially prepared) are enthusiastic and make buying decisions based on how a home makes them feel. If the crackle of the fireplace sends chills up their spine, I can relate. If they love the idea that the backyard is fenced so Fifi, their precious poodle, won't escape, I can empathize.

But it's much tougher for me to connect with a highly analytical buyer who says to his or her spouse, "We're not going to buy that other house you love with the fireplace because, based on my calculations, *this* house is worth 43 cents more per square foot!" Don't get me wrong: there's nothing wrong with this line of thinking. It's just tougher for me as a salesperson to understand where this buyer is coming from based on how I best communicate. And it's probably equally puzzling for such a buyer to understand me as well.

Have you ever gone to a store to make a big purchase like a car or a computer and decided not to buy because you weren't pleased with the salesperson? It may have appeared as though she didn't care, was aloof, speaking a language you couldn't understand? Chances are the two of you just weren't connecting in the sales-chemistry department!

How can homebuyers shop for a salesperson they'll not only feel comfortable with, but also one who will provide the services they need to smooth out the homebuying process? Let's tackle the first part of that question first.

To Find an Agent That You'll Feel Comfortable Working With

- Go back to an agent you've worked with successfully before. Chances are the fit was good and you'll be pleased again.
- Ask people you know who are similar to you in personality and values for a recommendation. Ask why they'd recommend that person as an agent (personal referrals are the number one marketing tool of a prosperous real estate professional).
- Talk to agents who are members of the same clubs, church organizations, and social gatherings you frequent. The adage "like likes like" applies here and may help you gravitate to an agent with interests similar to yours.
- If personal referrals aren't available, drive through a neighborhood you're considering and note which brokerages and agents have listings in that area. Many agents will sell properties in what they call *farm areas* (areas they specialize in), which may be near their own homes. Similar lifestyles can be a good common denominator.

- Look in the newspaper or other advertising publication to view properties in your price range (this is one of the benefits of being prequalified or preapproved). Note which brokerages and agents have the majority of listings; a wealth of salable inventory can be a strong sign of a progressive company.
- Decide if it's important that your agent belong to the professional trade association, the National Association of REALTORS®. As a REALTOR® member or associate, the agent is bound to a code of ethics, including guidelines for working with buyers and sellers. In addition, the buyer has recourse against the agent through a hearing panel of the agent's peers if these ethics are breached and the buyer is damaged. The REALTOR® trademark may appear on the agent's business cards and marketing materials. Additionally, you may benefit from working with agents who have professional designations from affiliated institutes of the National Association of REALTORS® such as GRI (Graduate, Realtors Institute) values and CRS (Certified Residential Specialist). This indicates that the agent values his education and consumers benefit from it.

If you've chosen someone to work with, IT'S YOUR MOVE ➤

 ## Select the Type of Agency Relationship You Desire

Along with finding an agent you're comfortable with, you need to match up the services you'll require with the services the agent provides. It's just as much a priority today for consumers to receive a high level of service in the homebuying process as it is to find a good comfort level with the agent they choose. Service levels have radically changed over the past several years not only because of consumer needs but because of issues over who represents whom.

To understand this (and the choices available to you), let's review the ways you could work with an agent.

The First Step: Agency Disclosure

Forty-eight states currently require some form of agency disclosure. As a buyer, this means that the agent must divulge the various ways you can work with him and his brokerage in the sale. This is necessary because an agent does not necessarily represent you and your interests in the purchase. In fact, as we'll see, traditionally the agent has represented the seller, *not* the buyer.

It's also important to note that when an agent explains the agency relationship he has with you, this is merely notification of the relationship. Depending on the selection you make, there may be additional paperwork involved to legally contract for the service you choose.

It will help you understand the relationship options if you consider that (unless a specific state law dictates otherwise), agents represent the broker they're licensed with and are legal extensions of that broker. While you may be working with one agent, you are really working with the brokerage at large.

The various types of services and working relationships you might be offered are described below.

1. Work with the agent as a customer.   This means that while the agent provides service and information to you, he legally represents the seller. This was the traditional and virtually the only way real estate was sold until approximately 12 years ago. Agents listed a seller's property and legally represented that seller. This relationship also extended to agents at other cooperating offices who might work with buyers (especially offices affiliated with the Multiple Listing Service—MLS—a compendium/database of listed properties). This means that if you purchased a home more than ten years ago, it is probable that the agent you worked with represented the seller.

Even though agents may have acted as though they represented the buyer, they were usually legal representatives of the seller. Many agents were confused about this and innocently provided client-level services to buyer customers in an effort to "get a sale for the seller." Confusing these services was neither legal nor ethical. The industry has since realized this and adjusted its practices for the most part.

If you choose to work as a customer, the agent can provide you with information about the marketplace, schools, and services but cannot interpret this information for you nor negotiate on your behalf. However, both the agent and the seller must disclose material facts and defects known about the property unless the state's laws prohibit them from doing so. These facts must be disclosed no matter what kind of working relationship you have. Another agency option is to—

2. Work with the agent as a client. This means that the agent legally represents you and provides both information and advocacy on your behalf. This level of service goes beyond information sharing. The agent actually becomes your advocate and can negotiate on your behalf as well as help interpret information for you. If you are a client, all information you share with the agent is kept confidential, including how much you'd be willing to pay for a property, your motivation to purchase, and your time frame to do so.

To achieve this relationship, you might be asked to sign a buyer agency agreement that is much like a seller's listing agreement. It states that the agent legally works for you and that, in return, you agree to work solely with him for a specified period of time. You would also need to divulge anything that could assist the agent in finding property for you, which could include detailed information about your financial situation and other confidential information.

While current national statistics show that 95 percent of buyer agents are paid through the transaction (traditionally what we've thought of as the selling portion of the fee paid by the seller in the transaction), the agreement you sign may also require you to pay the buyer agent's fee in the event payment is not authorized by the seller of the house you choose.

Here again, all material facts known about the property must be communicated to you. A third type of agency relationship would be to—

3. Work with the agent in a dual agency capacity. This means that the brokerage represents both you and the listed seller as a dual client. This most often occurs when you are working as a client with the agent and choose to view one of the brokerage's in-house listings. When working in dual agency, you give up some of the services previously exclusive to you as a sole client, because there are now two clients and only one brokerage represented in the transaction. This means that the brokerage and agent(s) involved take a neutral position between the parties and will communicate to the seller only the information you authorize.

An example would be the following: The house you're interested in is listed at $85,000. You initially offer $80,000, but would be willing to go up to $85,000 if you have to. That information would not be disclosed to the seller unless you gave the agent permission to do so.

To achieve this relationship, you would probably be asked to sign a disclosed dual agency agreement, specifying what services you would or would not receive under this relationship. The fourth option is to—

4. Work with the agent as a facilitator/transaction broker/ transaction coordinator.   If recognized by the state you're in, the agent can *assist* both parties but legally represent neither (this is called facilitator, transaction broker, contract broker, or transaction coordinator status depending on the state). The agent acts as an impartial third party, transmitting information between the parties while not negotiating for either. Think of him as an information source, much like an encyclopedia. As with any other working relationship you have with an agent, all material facts and defects must be disclosed by both the agent and the seller.

Do all of these options sound confusing? They don't need to. As the consumer you have the right to choose the type of working relationship you desire—the one that best suits your needs. This can also be based on the types of services available from the agent you've chosen and the practices of the brokerage.

Once you've decided on the type of agency relationship you want, IT'S YOUR MOVE ✄

 Determine If You Can Contract for Only the Real Estate Services You Need

Some brokerages and agents can provide individual à la carte services to assist you as a buyer. These services could include prequalifying, locating a specific property, consulting on buying problems, negotiating on your behalf, and bringing the sale to a successful close. While you can compensate the agent in a variety of ways, many agent consultants are paid hourly fees, not percentages of the purchase price. This is one way to select the expertise you need, when you need it. You can find agents who specialize in consulting work through the traditional channels mentioned previously or by searching the Yellow Pages of the phone book under the heading Real Estate Consultants.

In lieu of, or in addition to, the previous menu of services, you may want to explore available real estate in cyberspace. If so, IT'S YOUR MOVE ♣

 ## Use the Internet to Find Real Estate

Kiosks, or free-standing electronic information centers, started springing up across the country more than a decade ago. By touching a screen, they allowed consumers to view property available throughout the United States. Today that same concept is as close as your own PC as various online services allow you to access U.S. as well as international real estate.

You can begin your cyberspace real estate search in various ways. You can access a variety of bulletin board listings on America Online, Prodigy, and the Internet to locate property by yourself and/or with the aid of a real estate agent.

For example, in the Real Estate Online section of America Online (AOL), you can search for property by state, city, or according to other criteria such as seller financing available or number of bedrooms. Listings are posted by for-sale-by-owners and real estate agents alike, and they afford a great opportunity to find out information about prices and services in an area.

And in addition to actual property listings, there's a vast amount of consumer information on homebuying, financing, environmental concerns, and even how to apply for a loan online.

To give you an idea of what you'll find, let's walk through the home search process online.

Locating Property/Homebuying Information

http://www.realtorads.com   This home page of the National Association of REALTORS® contains more than 600,000 listings from more than 30 states. You can not only obtain facts about properties, but also see color snapshots. Appointments to view the homes would be made through REALTOR® members.

In addition, there's a section entitled Tips for Buying, Selling and Maintaining Your Home. It features questions and answers on a wide variety of real estate homebuying/selling topics with insight from national experts (me included!)—and it will link you directly to my home page: http://www.realtorads.com/consumer/juliebio.htm.

http://www.ired.com IRED is an exciting location with information about U.S. as well as international property, all with great links. (For example, you can view real estate in Australia and have a geography lesson at the same time.) IRED also includes classified ads for properties for sale or lease, as well as a listing of real estate services available from various sources. IRED rates real estate Web sites, too. This site is a must on your cyberspace spin.

inman.com If it's consumer real estate news you're after, this home page has it. Brad Inman, a real estate journalist from California, has put together a winning combination of current news, homebuying/selling tips, and real-estate-related articles. Updated daily, it's a great place to get the education you need to be an informed homebuyer.

http://www.reea.org The home page of the Real Estate Educators Association is full of facts for educators and consumers alike. You'll enjoy the articles, the updates on topics like finance and law—always timely, always insightful. (Being a past president of the organization, I could be a bit biased!)

http://www.comspace.com If you're looking for commercial real estate in one of 28 major cities across the U.S., Comspace has it, complete with local market information and property available for lease and for sale. It's a great way to get up to speed on what's happening in commercial real estate.

http://www.by-owner.com This is a FSBO (for sale by owner) site with listings in 33 states. You can read the ad and then contact the owner by calling a toll-free number.

http://www.owners.com   Another FSBO home page, this one is very user-friendly and encompasses more than 6,300 homes in 48 states. Sellers are offered a free listing with a lot of room for explaining the home's amenities and can include a picture.

Locating Financing Information and Options

http://www.hsh.com/   HSH, Inc., is a financial information company well known for its current information on rates, indices, and financial trends. (You may remember hearing about their great ARM rate adjustment checking kit.) This is a great place to go to check out current terms for adjustable rate mortgages or get a feel for where interest rates may be going.

http://www.countrywide.com   This large national mortgage company not only provides current mortgage rates and available programs, but also lets you shop for a mortgage using one of two approaches: a quick application (that will tell you how much home you can afford) and a longer application (similar to the formal one you'd do for a loan application). Either way, you can earmark your visit by obtaining a transit number and then if you ever want to apply directly for a loan with Countrywide, you won't have to duplicate the information. You can also shop for insurance service online.

http://www.mortgage-mart.com   This site provides a wide array of real estate articles, market updates, and prequalifying information. In addition, you can input information on a mortgage application form and have your loan "shopped" with several lenders to find the best loan.

http://www.fanniemae.com/   Fannie Mae (FNMA), the largest purchaser of loans from lenders, has pulled together an incredible compendium of consumer information to help you with your homebuying expedition. There's a bilingual glossary of real estate terms, information on how to purchase FNMA foreclosed homes, and a complete rundown of all the mortgage programs available to the lender from Fannie Mae.

Environmental Information

http://www.nsc.org/nsc/ehc/ehc.html National Lead Information Center. This home page contains an abundance of information on lead-based paint and lead poisoning. It can link you to information on radon, air quality, and other environmental health issues.

Other Real Estate Information Sources

http://www.cswv.com/consumer Case Shiller Weiss is a statistical services company that estimates home values based on a specific street address. Property Valuation Service has been used by banks, insurance companies, and other financial institutions and is now available to consumers. By contacting them online with the street address of the property you're interested in, they can use their extensive database of information to give you an estimate of the property's value. There is a charge for the service and it is currently only available in ten states.

http://www.real-estate-ed.com The home page of the Real Estate Education Company lets you browse its electronic bookshelves for other books you need to make your homebuying journey a smooth one, get information on starting your real estate or insurance career, or review cutting-edge information on just what's happening in real estate education.

These are just a few of the exciting locations for real estate information in cyberspace.

Cautions about "Surfing the Web" for a House

Now that you see how easy it is to access homebuying information at your fingertips, you may need to ask even more questions before you leap into using the information. For example, will it save me money to use this information? And what are the pros and cons of using electronic information to purchase a home?

Regarding the ability to save money using the Internet, it depends. If you're one of those Lone Wolf purchasers we talked about previously and you have enough savvy to shop for the services you need, you might find discounted fee services (like mortgages) through the Internet. But if you're a Red Riding Hood buyer who gets cold feet just thinking about piecing a sale together by yourself, it may actually end up costing you more money.

In addition, be careful about sharing your name, Social Security number, address, and phone number online. Most lenders who use online services to gather introductory information from potential customers agree that the Internet is primarily a way to make the initial contact with the customer, not sign and seal the loan application. If you're like many borrowers who want to guard personal information, make sure to give only your screen (online) name and then have the service provider contact you for a face-to-face or phone-to-phone contact.

As with any source of data, you need to thoroughly check out the source and the information before taking any action. This is particularly true of real estate on the Internet, since there is no one sole source for inputting (or policing) the information, it's not verified before being placed in cyberspace, and, just as in any other business arena, you might come across an occasional scam.

Here's an approach that should help you to verify the validity of the information you find. First, know who placed the information there. If it's placed by an owner, is the owner willing to back up the information with a seller's disclosure sheet about the property? What supporting data did the seller consult before "listing" the property online (e.g., comparative market analysis, appraisal, home inspection)?

If the property ad was placed by an agent, what additional information is the agent willing to share with you? Is there additional printed information you can receive such as a seller's disclosure sheet or a formal Multiple Listing Service information sheet?

Only in very rare cases do buyers purchase property sight unseen over the Internet. Until you get an opportunity to "kick the tires" and confirm the data, treat what you gather as preliminary information.

No matter to what degree you apply data available in cyberspace, you must agree it's given us a wealth of real estate information—just by being able to point and click!

In addition to the exciting world of cyberspace, you may want to try your hand at working with unlisted FSBOs. If so, IT'S YOUR MOVE ♠

 ## Decide If FSBO Homes Are a Possibility

We would be remiss if we didn't spend time on the special challenge posed by working with for-sale-by-owners (FSBOs). These are generally well-meaning folks who just want to sell their house. But often their apparent lack of information about the homebuying market and/or the sales process can create challenging roadblocks for the homebuyer!

There are a variety of reasons why people choose to sell their homes themselves. Owners might

1. feel that no one knows more about the house than they do;
2. have the time necessary to spend on marketing, screening buyers, showing the property, and troubleshooting the sale;
3. have had a previous adverse experience with an agent or other real estate professional; or
4. feel that by selling the house themselves, they maintain control of the sale while saving the real estate commission. (We probably should have used this as the #1 reason!)

The following are keys to working successfully with a FSBO.

First, try to understand the FSBOs' mindset. Any or all of the rationales mentioned above may be part of their agenda.

Second, try to determine their "hot buttons." What is most important to them? Is it a quick sale or getting full price for their property? While it's sometimes difficult to pinpoint the prime motivation, spending time getting inside their heads and hearts will often give you the insight you need.

Third, if at all possible, use a third party to negotiate the sale. Most of us who have negotiated for ourselves realize too late the impact of the third-party advocate. (In fact, for the last property my husband and I purchased, we used a buyer's agent to represent us. I know from past experience that I typically leave too much on the table and end up shorting myself in the process, trying to overkill in fairness!) Even if you've decided not to work with an agent to locate property for you, you will be light-years ahead using an agent to negotiate on your behalf with a FSBO.

One additional benefit of using a third-party advocate is that the agent can pull together comparable sales statistics, or "comps," of houses that have sold in the area similar to the one you're interested in. This can help you rest easier that you aren't overpaying for the house. (We'll cover specific tips for successful negotiating in Step #7.)

Okay, if you want to buy from a FSBO and you don't want a third party to negotiate for you, at least do one thing: use professional services to check out the property. Nightmare situations can result from a buyer who relies on property representations (albeit innocent) from the seller, only to find major discrepancies after closing. The precarious combination of the naive buyer and the unknowledgeable seller can be deadly without input from a third-party professional! (Note: A qualified inspector doesn't include your Uncle Harold who once lived in a house with electricity—use a professional home inspector or other specialist to do the job!)

If you've mastered all six challenges of "Find the Help You Need," then congratulations, IT'S YOUR MOVE to Homebuying Step #6 ⬥

But if you've fallen short in a few areas, GO TO THE PENALTY BOX.

Penalty Box

Possible penalties include the following:

1. Getting in the middle of a transaction and realizing that you need help completing it
2. Feeling uncomfortable with a certain level of real estate service and not asking for additional or different services from the agent
3. Wanting to "surf the Net" for homebuying information, but not knowing where to go or how to go about it

For "help" out of the PENALTY BOX:

1. Decide which homebuying profile you fit (Red Riding Hood or Lone Wolf) and determine what help you'll need.
2. Interview several agents to see how the "fit" will be if you work together.
3. Get acquainted with how the Internet can assist your homebuying adventure (even if it is only for the articles and homebuying tips).

 Take Trump Card #5

Analyze what level and type of help you need in your homebuying quest. It's no longer a "one size fits all" buying world, so it makes sense to seek out specific services that meet your needs, rendered by the most suitable person to work with you. Don't settle for less.

Step 6

Choose the Best House

Do you believe it? We're actually ready to look at houses! But before we do (you knew there was a hitch), decide what you're looking for so you'll know the right house once you find it.

Make a "Wish List"

The best way to decide which features are most important in your new house is to make a "wish list." Obviously, this list should reflect not only what you want, but also what you can afford. For example, if I'm buying a home in Chicago and I'm preapproved for a $50,000 loan, chances are pretty good that I can scratch an Olympic-size swimming pool from my list!

Here's a system that works well to help you rank your options. Figure 6.1, Home "Wish List," shows a number of features and amenities. The first time you go through the list, mark a "1" beside each item that you "would like to have." The second time through the list, mark a "2" beside each item that you "have

FIGURE 6.1 Home "Wish List"

The first time through this checklist, mark a "1" next to the items you would "LIKE TO HAVE" in a home. The second time through the list, concentrate only on the items you checked before, and add a "2" next to each item that you "HAVE TO HAVE." Then tally up each individual score. The items with the "3's" become the mandatory features; the balance of the amenities are nice, but not necessary.

Final step: Go back through the items that scored a "3" and rank them by their importance. That way you'll know which amenities are most important when househunting.

	Like to Have	Have to Have	Total Score	Top Priorities
Type of home				
1. Condo	___	___	___	___
2. Town house	___	___	___	___
3. Detached single family	___	___	___	___
4. Other (specify)	___	___	___	___
Type of neighborhood				
1. Describe (e.g., rural, urban, close to shopping, close to schools, etc.)	___	___	___	___
2. Describe	___	___	___	___
Architectural style and design				
1. Describe (e.g., colonial, single level, ranch with basement, new construction, etc.)	___	___	___	___
2. Describe	___	___	___	___
Interior features				
1. No. of bedrooms	___	___	___	___
2. No. of bathrooms	___	___	___	___
3. Separate dining room	___	___	___	___
4. Family room	___	___	___	___
5. Office room	___	___	___	___
6. Basement (if applicable)	___	___	___	___
7. Lots of cupboard space	___	___	___	___
8. Fireplace	___	___	___	___
Exterior features				
1. Size of lot	___	___	___	___
2. Attached garage	___	___	___	___
3. Detached garage	___	___	___	___
4. Storage shed, etc.	___	___	___	___
Other features you feel are important (specify) ___	___	___	___	___
___	___	___	___	___

to have." Then tally up each individual score. The items with the 3s become the mandatory features; the balance become nice, but not necessary.

Next, go back to the items that scored a "3" and rank their order of importance. That way you'll know which amenities are most imported when you go househunting. And then be prepared to give up even some of those! The house selection process is full of trade-offs!

Some of you may be asking, what happens if I don't know what I want? Use contrary thinking. Come up with answers based on what you *don't want,* and work back from there. This process often works well because most of us have lived in houses or apartments that were less than ideal. Remember the kitchen so small you had to step into the living room to crack an egg?

I may know that I don't want to spend all weekend mowing the lawn, but I also don't want to be sharing a common wall with someone else in a condominium development. Probably a detached house on a small lot, maybe in a planned unit development, would work for me.

If you have trouble knowing exactly what you want, use the checklist to cross off what you don't want, then work with the remainder. If you've got your wish list in mind, then IT'S YOUR MOVE ✦

 ## Make Sure the House Matches Your Lifestyle

No matter what interior amenities you shoot for, make sure they're in the right package. A house is more than brick and mortar; it serves as a nucleus for the lifestyle you choose.

This is one reason why some buyers today rank their outside living areas higher than their inside space. For example, a golf course within walking distance might not be important to me, but could be the primary reason why an avid golfer (like my banker) buys in a neighborhood.

I once sold a town house to a woman who just "had to have one." Much of her motivation was that it was in vogue at the time (mid-1980s) and several of her friends had them. She thought she was buying a unique configuration of four walls when in fact she was really buying a different lifestyle—one that did not fit her tastes.

I ended up relisting and selling the town house in three months. But unfortunately she lost money selling so soon after she had purchased.

New or Resale?

Depending on where you live and the price of the house you can afford, it may not be much of a decision whether to go with new or resale construction. But let's assume that you haven't been priced out of the new home market and let's weigh the pros and cons of each.

New homes are wonderful—clean and sparkling, pristine carpet and linoleum, with everything smelling so fresh. And new homes are horrible—grass to plant, curtains (and drapery rods) to purchase, and usually at least one glitch (albeit minor) to repair.

 A national survey recently found that the owner of a new home spends an average of $6,000 the first year on additions of personal property and property fixtures. And that's an average figure.

The first new house I had was a real challenge. Not only did I find that the doors were hung improperly, the windows were so cheap that the condensation in the winter made it look like it was raining—inside!

And then there was the yard: a third of an acre of weeds. Three years later when I sold that house, there were still some weeds at the back of the lot tall enough to lose a small child in.

But there are benefits to owning a newly constructed home. First, if the home is covered by a home owner's warranty, a majority of repair costs will be covered. Programs such as the well-known Home Owner's Warranty (HOW) provide a ten-year extended warranty. Obviously, there will be fewer costs in general because the home is new. Some recurring costs like home owner's insurance and utilities should be less because the property is new and built under energy-efficienct guidelines.

The preowned home has positives, too. The landscaping is in, the window coverings are in place (and paid for), and there's a track record for things like how much it costs to heat, cool, and maintain the house. (If the seller won't share information on the utility costs with you, you can usually obtain that information from the utility company.)

Preowned homes usually cost less per square foot to purchase, so you may be able to buy more home for your money, especially if square footage is a high priority on your list. And you'll often hear buyers remark that they can see what kind of neighborhood they're buying into when they purchase a resale home, whereas the environment of the new subdivision is still under development.

But you only have to be saddled buying one "lemon" house to know that the wrong resale home can end up costing you a bundle in maintenance and repairs. Thus, the debate about new construction versus preowned continues.

The Decision to Custom Build Your Dream Home

I must admit, although I've purchased a handful of homes, I've never had one custom-built, nor have I had the desire to. Why? Because I know I would drive myself (or the contractor) crazy before it was completed. Patience is not one of my biggest virtues.

But that doesn't mean that *you* shouldn't take the custom-home plunge. It may make sense if there's nothing like what you want on the market. Just be careful not to invent something that no one else would want either! Or it may make sense if you've already invested in a lot and want to build your dream home on it. But we could fill up the balance of the book with precautions you should take if you custom build your home—everything from choosing the general contractor and the best financing to coping with time and cost overruns. The key is to know and trust the people you're dealing with; but reduce everything, and I do mean *everything*, to writing.

Choose a Home to Fit Your Lifestyle

To help ensure that your style of living matches the house you're seeking, think about the following before you begin house-hunting:

Condominium or town house lifestyle

- A smaller yard with potentially less yard work
- Closer neighbors than with single-family detached homes

- Monthly payments for maintenance and upkeep of the association
- Possible use of a common area, which could include pool, tennis courts, activity center

Multifamily unit (like a duplex or triplex) lifestyle

- Closer neighbors
- The need to serve as a landlord in renting the other units
- Someone close by to watch your home when you're not there

Mobile home lifestyle

- The ability to relocate your home
- A low-maintenance yard
- Paying lot rent if you don't own your own land

Home-in-the-city lifestyle

- A shorter commute (if you work in the city)
- Less elbow room than in the country
- A shorter distance to shopping and other amenities
- Higher property taxes due to the greater amount of city services provided

Home in the country (or outlying urban part of the county) lifestyle

- A longer commute (if you work in the city)
- More elbow room than in the city (which could include a larger parcel of land)
- Greater costs of accessing shopping and other amenities
- Lower property taxes due to lack of services provided

All lifestyles are a matter of trade-offs, aren't they? Just make sure the type of structure you choose aptly reflects the lifestyle you enjoy and/or seek. If you've chosen the type of home style *and* lifestyle you think you'll enjoy, then IT'S YOUR MOVE

Choose the Right Neighborhood

Never has it been more important than it is right now to scrutinize the neighborhood when house hunting, not only to retain your home's investment value, but also for your peace of mind.

Just as you did when selecting the amenities you wanted in your house, its location and neighborhood have as much to do with your comfort as what's inside.

That's why we've provided the following resources to get answers to your questions in evaluating the neighborhood.

Gather Neighborhood Information by "Driving Around"

1. Does the traffic flow easily near the property or are there bottle necks, especially in accessing main arterial streets? (In addition to slowing you down, traffic jams can cause excessive noise and noxious fumes near the property.) Make sure you drive to and from the house during at least one workday and also one weekend day. It's amazing how traffic volume can change!

2. Check the commute (and time it), but obviously not on Sunday! If the distance will drastically increase over your present circumstances, be sure to consider the added cost, including time away from home and any additional child care expense involved.

3. Take different routes to the property, not just the standard approach via the main street. Are there any unsightly areas you've missed such as dumpsites and factories bordering the property?

4. Take a test run to places you frequent, such as your child's school, Little League practice field, and the babysitter's. If this location poses added driving time, you need to be able to deal with it.

Gather Neighborhood Information by "Walking Around"

1. Stroll up the street to check for noise pollution and other noxious sounds. Can you hear a whirring table saw and whining router in the handy-man garage two doors away? Does one neighbor have more than his share of barking dogs? What about fencing between neighbors? Are animals running loose? Are leaves blowing, accumulating from the street behind the house you're considering?

2. Scrutinize the air quality. Can you detect odor from any processing plants or other manufacturing companies? Is the house located an adequate distance from any agricultural concerns, like feed lots or stock sales yards? (This will affect the home's resale value as well.)

3. Check the condition of the streets and sidewalks. Does there appear to be adequate drainage? Are streets and driveways cracked and in a state of disrepair? Are parking areas free of debris? (Note: Crumbling sidewalks could signal that repair work is needed and a local improvement district assessment might be levied to fund the work. This could mean additional annual costs to you if you purchase this property.)

4. Lighting is a big concern today. Check not only the neighborhood street lighting, but also exterior lighting on the house you're considering. (You'd obviously have to do this at night.) Is there adequate lighting from any parking area to home entrances like the front door and garage walkway? Is the lighting visible from the street, and are porches well lit (and free from obstructions like shrubs and trees)? If large additional lighting poles are positioned on the property, find out if you pay or if the cost is shared by several neighbors.

5. Finally, but perhaps most important, check the property for safety. Neighborhood safety factors are a prime concern for homebuyers today. Purchasing a home in an unsafe area not only affects your property value but your peace of mind as well. And while you may think it's tough getting information about the types and frequency of crime in a neighborhood, there are statistics available for your review.

- Is the neighborhood safe? Just as you checked in and around the house for safety concerns, find out how safe the area is before purchasing. The safety information officer of the local police department will be able to give you information about crime in the area once you give the officer the names of the cross streets nearest the property.

The statistics may be broken down into the type, amount, and frequency of crimes. And while the information won't guarantee that the neighborhood is safe, it is a good indication of trends and can alert you to what precautions you should take.

In addition, you can ask the information officer at the police department about any Crime Watch groups in the neighborhood you're considering. Many cities have area-wide programs, broken down into various geographic areas.

- Make note of areas close to the home with vacated or burned-out buildings, razed building sites, or other areas that could be unsafe. This is particularly important if you have small children who may be lured to them as a play area.
- If you haven't already done so, check the zoning of adjacent areas around the neighborhood you're considering. Have there been any recent changes, or are changes pending that could affect your neighborhood? Zoning downgrades on neighboring property can not only change property values but create an increase in crime, especially if the property is for a nonresidential use.

Gather Information by "Asking Around"

People to contact.   People with information about neighborhoods include:

- Real estate agents
- Appraisers/assessors
- Property managers
- Bankers/lenders

- Title insurance professionals
- Real estate attorneys
- Utility company repair people, phone installers, and delivery people
- Postal employees in the area

Why talk to this selection of people? Because their careers revolve around working with or accessing real estate in some way.

But the very best source of the information you need often comes from neighbors currently living in an area. If the opportunity is available, make personal contacts with the neighbors. It may prove to be one of the best upfront and specific sources of information.

Current residents—your best source of information. Ask current residents the following questions:

1. Would they buy there again? If not, why not?
2. Have they tried to sell their property? If so, why didn't it sell? If they haven't tried, do they think they would have any trouble selling it? If so, why?
3. Do they feel the area is generally quiet? If no, why not? (Any specific concerns?)
4. How have property values fared in the last several years? Have assessed values gone up, down, or stayed the same?
5. What is the mix of renters to owner-occupants in the area?
6. Are the schools of good quality? Why or why not?
7. Have they seen much crime or vandalism in the neighborhood? If so, was police and ambulance response timely and satisfactory?
8. Where do they shop near the area and why?

It's wise to gather information from several residents, not just one or two, so that your overview won't be slanted nor biased. Remember, the seller of the property you're interested in may be biased. It's best to get a cross section of answers from neighbors to help you evaluate the neighborhood. If you feel good about what you've gathered so far, IT'S YOUR MOVE

Gather Property Information by "Checking Around"

Unless prohibited by the laws of the state in which you're purchasing, the real estate agent you're working with must disclose all material facts to you about the property. In addition, if you're purchasing a home in one of 12 different states, the seller is required to provide you with a seller's disclosure statement. This form is a checklist of information about the property (to the best of the seller's knowledge.) Most of these states require the seller to fill out the form and sign it so that the information provided is deemed to come directly from the seller. But don't think that the seller is actually warranting the condition. Facts are a start, but a warranty is an entirely different matter.

Even if your state doesn't have this seller disclosure rule, you can ask the agent and/or the seller to provide you with such a disclosure.

If you're working on your own, *do not* make an offer before obtaining a seller disclosure form or at least checking out the facts. You may be saddled with a property that is either not soundly constructed or a time bomb waiting to fall apart (usually immediately after closing!).

Since not required in all states as material facts that must be disclosed, investigate if any violent crimes, such as murder or rape, have occurred on the property. The biggest concern is typically that after purchase you might not be able to resell the property. You also need to consider the psychological impact that a crime of this nature might have on your mental well-being.

What to Find Out about the Property

1. Check the general soundness of the property's exterior and interior.
2. Check the electrical and mechanical systems. This means that you should test the working condition of each item; for example, turn on the air-conditioning in the dead of winter and the furnace in the dog days of summer. Don't forget attic fans, air cleaners, window air conditioners, and sprinkler systems. If it's got a switch, turn it on! Service stickers on furnaces and air-conditioning units may give

indicate when they were last serviced or note any problems the owners were having with the equipment.

Don't forget to flush toilets and turn on faucets, noting any leaks, slow-running drains, and/or inadequate water pressure.

While most potential buyers don't do it, it's good to test several (if not all) electrical outlets throughout the house. (It's not unusual for older homes to have burned-out outlets or entire walls with no electricity because of broken wires.)

3. Don't forget to check the appliances that stay with the house. Check age, quality, and turn them all on. Ask the seller if warranty information is available on newer appliances.

4. The general condition of the house's interior should be noted. Pay special attention to potential trouble areas, such as brown spots (water) on the ceiling or near plumbing, blistered wall coverings or paint (that could signal a leaky roof), and sloping floors or repaired and replaced floor covering.

5. Don't forget to journey to the crawl space and the attic. I know no one likes to do this, but you can tell if there's dampness (a sign of leakage) and if insulation is adequate. In addition, a look in the attic might warn you of roof problems and/or leaks around the chimney area where flashing has worked loose and rain is coming in.

While many wise buyers want their offers contingent upon obtaining an acceptable home inspection by a professional inspector, doing the initial walk-through we've outlined will give you a good idea of problem areas you may encounter.

One last suggestion: Don't get emotionally swept away by the gleam of the imported ceramic countertops or the highly buffed hardwood floors. Look beneath the obvious to determine if this house is a sound *and* safe investment. If the information you gathered is adequate, but you still want reassurance about the property's soundness, then IT'S YOUR MOVE

Evaluate Property Soundness with a Home Inspection

If it's been over more than five years since you've bought a property, you may not have had the benefit of a home inspection. Not only is this a burgeoning new industry, but it can afford you some peace of mind about the physical soundness of the biggest financial purchase you may ever make.

In most cases, the home inspection takes place after the purchase agreement is signed. Making your offer contingent upon receiving a satisfactory inspection report is advisable. (In the future, inspections are likely to occur *before* the property is placed on the market since the turnaround time for closing may be reduced to days—if not hours!) We want to tackle the basics of home inspection here in case you're tempted to go it alone without one (not the best advice), and hopefully convince you that sidestepping one is not in your best interests.

Let's get you comfortable with what will happen during the home inspection, who the players are, and what to do with the information that's uncovered.

It's imperative that the person doing the home inspection have nothing to gain by finding things wrong with the house. So if the prospective inspector you call says, "Yes, I do general contracting as well," choose someone else!

Before you select an inspector through the Yellow Pages of the phone book, ask lenders and other real estate professionals who they'd recommend. Although there is no national licensing or sanctioning agency for home inspectors (but several states do certify them), one benchmark of quality is an inspector who is a member of the American Society of Home Inspectors (ASHI). Not only does this society provide continuing education for inspectors, each society member is required to complete a minimum of 250 paid inspections, pass a rigorous examination, and adhere to a professional code of ethics.

Ask the inspector if he is bonded and has liability insurance. Also ask for personal references (other than real estate agents and lenders) from homebuyers he's worked for.

If at all possible, accompany the inspector as he reviews the property. You'll be amazed at what you'll learn about construction as well as tips for improving and weatherizing the home. If you're paying for this service (since most buyers do pick up the bill for the home inspection, which is about $200 to $500), you may as well get your money's worth.

In addition to the major areas of the home, a full home inspection will include investigation into the following possibilities:

Radon.   Found in most rocks and soils, radon is an odorless, colorless radioactive gas that is a byproduct of uranium when it breaks down. Outdoors, it mixes with air and is harmless, but trapped inside a house, it can reach toxic concentrations. In fact, a high level of radon in a home can cause cancer in humans.

Radon testing can be done with do-it-yourself test kits; however, unless it is done properly, the results may not be accurate. Quality testing is best left to a home inspector, because one in five homes may show some trace of radon.

Improving ventilation in a home usually solves most radon problems. This could include venting crawl spaces and/or adding fans for better air circulation.

Lead poisoning/lead-based paint.   Approximately three-quarters of the nation's housing stock built before 1978 contains some lead-based paint, which has contributed to more than one million children with blood-lead levels above safe limits. Lead poisoning can cause permanent damage to the brain and other organs.

Based on these statistics, federal law now requires the disclosure of known information on lead-based paint and lead-based paint hazards before the sale or lease of most housing built before 1978.

What is required:

- Before ratification of a contract for a housing sale, sellers must disclose known lead-based paint and provide reports to buyers.
- Sellers must give buyers the pamphlet entitled "Protect Your Family from Lead in Your Home."
- Homebuyers will get a ten-day period to conduct a lead-based paint inspection at their own expense. Key terms of the evaluation can be negotiated between the parties.
- Sales contracts must include certain notification and disclosure language.

- In addition, sellers and real estate agents share responsibility for ensuring compliance.

(The foregoing conditions apply equally to rental units except housing for the elderly or handicapped as long as no children live there.)

What is not required:

- Sellers are not required to test for or remove lead-based paint.
- No sales contract will be invalidated by the lead-based paint rule.

Effective dates:

- For properties of more than four dwelling units, disclosure is effective September 6, 1996.
- For properties of four or fewer dwelling units, disclosure is effective December 6, 1996.

For a copy of the brochure "Protect Your Family from Lead in Your Home," call the National Lead Information Clearinghouse at 1-800-424-LEAD; or fax your request to 202-659-1192, or Internet e-mail to ehc@cais.com.

Asbestos.   Asbestos is a fireproof material that was used in a myriad of building materials (like insulation) prior to 1975. As the material breaks down, tiny fibers fly off, becoming airborne, and they can cause lung cancer. If you're looking at older homes, you can often find asbestos problems if insulation-wrapped water and heat pipes are unraveling.

Not all standard home inspections include searching for asbestos. Make sure yours does.

Formaldehyde.   In the same time-use category as asbestos is that of urea formaldehyde. You may remember it as the foam insulation used in the ceilings and walls of homes. It can emit noxious odors and the fumes can cause nausea and vomiting. Its use is banned throughout most of the United States, and homes where it is found may have trouble reselling because of it.

Again, you're best served to ask the inspector to put this on his list since it's not always a typical checklist item.

Termites.   Living in South Florida for several years, I came to recognize these little critters and the severe damage they can do. Although the majority of homes affected are more than five years old, it can happen in newer homes where the ground has not been properly treated at the time of construction.

If you or the inspector senses that there is infestation, it's recommended that you contact an exterminator for a thorough analysis of the damage. In many parts of the country, a termite inspection is mandatory for closing a mortgage loan.

Carpenter ants.   Another type of bug, another type of damage. Although they are a little easier to spot than termites, carpenter ants can hollow out wood in no time flat!

Dry rot.   Caused by water, poor ventilation, and other types of environmental damage, dry rot is another hazard that mortgage lenders will want reports on before closing a mortgage.

Water.   Because water can contain high levels of lead (as well as bacteria), having your source of water tested is an excellent idea, especially if it's well or spring water. Call your county service or extension service to obtain a test kit that you can use yourself and take a sample to the county office for testing. The charge is nominal.

 Search the Public Records for Additional Property Information

Check the public records in the county courthouse. Although the title report you receive at closing will reflect some of the information, you need to know about other items that may not show on the title report. These could include current or pending assessments for new streets, sidewalks, or sewer improvements. Payments on these levies would be your responsibility once you've closed the sale. If you're working with a real estate agent, he/she should provide this information to you.

Check with either the county courthouse or the title company if you have any questions regarding the property's legal description. Again, this will be noted in your title insurance policy at closing. But if you have any questions about physical matters such as fence lines, lot size, or easements, you should check these out immediately with the title company. A full survey prior to closing could be in order. If you've met the challenges of inspecting the property, then IT'S YOUR MOVE ♠

 **Evaluate the Schools**

High on the list of reasons for "why we chose this area" is generally the quality of the schools located there. And it's not just for folks who have children attending. Purchasing a home in a quality school district is a good ace in the hole for resale potential. Properties in school districts with good scholastic standing tend to appreciate in value. So even if your kids are out of the nest and you aren't worried about choosing a school, still gravitate to areas with quality schools since it may be money in your resale pocket!

Ask these questions:

1. Which schools would the kids attend?   This can be a tricky question since school district boundaries can change overnight. Your best bet is to contact the school administration office for information. You can ask to receive a letter confirming the schools for the area as of the current date. Again, the closer it gets to the time for a new school year, the more accurate the information will be.

2. What about the school's scholastic rating?   Most schools (or the local school administration office) should be glad to share information on how their schools fare in scholastic ratings (i.e., ACT/SAT testing). While it's certainly not the sole gauge of a school's quality, many parents feel it is a fair indication of the type of education their children will receive. In addition, you may want to ask the school administration office what the student-to-teacher ratio is for the school you're considering as well as for each grade your children will enroll in.

Make Sure the House Is Properly Priced

If you can master this challenge, you'll be money ahead not only when you buy, but also when you sell. In fact, an old real estate adage says, "You don't make money when you sell real estate, you make it when you *buy!*" If you buy an overpriced home, you may still be paying for it (literally) when you sell.

How can you tell that you're not overpaying for a house? If you're getting a mortgage on the property, some of this guesswork will be alleviated by the appraisal the lender will require.

But rather than waste your time and effort falling in love with and making an offer on a house that will never be appraised for what you're anticipating, here are some steps you can take *before* you make an offer.

1. Check out what other properties have sold for.   As mentioned previously, the selling prices of other properties with similar amenities in similar neighborhoods are good indicators of what the subject property (the house you're considering) is worth. Similar properties that have recently sold are called comparables or "comps" and are part of a formal comparison called a comparative market analysis or CMA. (See Figure 6.2 for a sample CMA form.) Preparing one is standard procedure for listing agents working with sellers and is a service provided to buyers working with buyers' agents. And although a real estate agent will prepare comps for you as a buyer/customer, the agent cannot legally interpret the information for you.

For example, the agent would not provide a buyer/customer with interpretations such as the cost per square foot of the various comps or comparisons about how the types of financing used made a difference in the price. This means that if you're working with an agent who is not representing you as a client, you may need additional help deciphering the comparable information you receive. (This is one reason why many buyers are choosing to have buyer agents represent them.)

You can get an overview of comps in one of two ways. The first, and most reliable, approach is to ask a real estate agent to prepare comps for you. Why is that information better? First, it comes from a central source of information, the Multiple Listing Service (MLS). Most Boards of REALTORS® are connected to the

FIGURE 6.2 Comparative Market Analysis

EWM
Esslinger • Wooten • Maxwell
Realtors®
Competitive Market Analysis

Associate ____________
Office Phone ____________ After Hours Phone ____________
Date ____________

Comp #	Address	19__ Assessed Value	Bedrooms/ Baths/ Garage	Year Built	Lot Size	Date of Sale	Listing Price	Sale Price	Adjusted Square Foot Area	Price Per Square Foot	Features Adjustment + or -
	Subject Property					X	X	X		X	
	Recently Sold										
	Currently for Sale										

Only you can set the price for your property, but to aid you in your decision, we have researched the current real estate market and offer the above information for your review. This is intended to be an estimate of value and not intended to create an Agency relationship.

Suggested Price Range $ ____________ **to $** ____________

Used with permission of EWM REALTORS®, Coral Gables, Florida.

MLS, making it a great repository of information for a large portion of your area. In addition, the agent has information at her fingertips to compare the subject property with others currently on the market, as well as with listings that expired and did not sell.

Second, you could gather the comparable information yourself. This can be time consuming and the information you obtain may not be the most accurate.

For example, you could contact owners with Sold signs in their yards, asking what they sold for, the terms and conditions of the sale, etc. Yes, you may get some feedback, but there is no guarantee that the information is correct or unbiased. (To save face, sellers are notorious for claiming, "Yes, I got my price," when in fact, "their price" was amended downward several times before they sold!)

2. Check out the homes currently listed that are similar to the one you're considering.
Know the listed prices of the competition as well as the terms they're offering. How does the house you're considering compare in types of financing and other terms?

If you're working on your own, you can gather addresses from real estate signs near the subject property, note the signs, and call to gather information.

3. Check the county assessor's office for assessed value.
Each property will have an assessed value posted in the county assessor's office. The key is in knowing the relationship between market value and assessed value. For example, the assessor will tell you that in our county, assessed value typically runs 75 percent of market value. That's an indication that if $75,000 is the assessed value for the property, it could bring more than $100,000 in a sale.

Don't forget to ask when the property was last assessed as well as check out other similar properties on the assessment rolls to see if their values correspond.

4. Ask an insurance agent what properties are worth in that area.
Even though they aren't real estate professionals, insurance agents may write a lot of residential business in an area and will have an idea of value. They can tell you such things as replacement value per square foot, lot value, and even informa-

tion about fire protection in an area. And because they err on the side of caution so as not to overinsure a property, the "guesstimate" you receive may be on the conservative side. Don't overlook this valuable source of information when you're trying to determine value.

5. Get an appraisal upfront—before you make an offer. Some buyers won't make an offer before they have an appraisal in their hot little hands. But this is not always an advisable or a prudent way to determine value.

Here's why. An appraisal by definition is one person's (the appraiser's) estimate of value. That estimate is typically set by "what a ready, willing, and able buyer will pay for a property." Until such a buyer has made a bona fide offer, it's tough for the appraiser to determine market value. That can often mean that the appraisal you get before an offer is made may be lower than what the buyer might pay and/or the market might bear.

Here's another concern. If the seller gets an appraisal upfront, it might not be needed (if the property sells for cash) or usable (if the property sells with FHA or VA financing and the conventional appraisal secured upfront won't work).

That's why it's generally in everyone's best interest to let a CMA set the stage for market value and hold off on an appraisal until a viable offer comes in.

The one exception to this rule might be if the seller has a specialty property that is unique in style, design, and amenities for the area. It might be difficult for the seller (and/or agent) to determine market value since few (if any) comps could be found. In this case, an upfront appraisal might be wise.

If you have a fairly good idea that the property is properly priced, then IT'S YOUR MOVE

 ## Safeguards to Prevent You from Paying Too Much

1. Be sure that any offer you make is contingent upon receiving an appraisal for at least the amount of the purchase price. That way, if the house doesn't appraise for that price, you won't have to buy and your earnest money

deposit will be refunded (if the purchase agreement is written that way).

2. Many buyers today are not just relying on an appraisal, but a combination of a satisfactory appraisal *and* home inspection. Once the appraisal is complete and a professional home inspector has viewed the property, you will feel much more secure knowing the house is fairly sound and worth the price.

If you understand the safeguards you can use, then IT'S YOUR MOVE ♠

 ## Evaluate Resale Potential *before* You Buy

This is a critical area, especially if you know you're going to be a short-term owner of the house. Many buyers overlook this challenge, and later suffer financial consequences that can't be undone at that point.

How can you evaluate resale potential before you buy? Here are some suggestions:

1. What has recently sold in the area? (We're back to the CMA and information you've gathered again!) How long did it take them to sell? Were there drastic price reductions (based on both the listed price and what other houses in comparable markets are selling for)?

2. Check how the sold comps have been financed. Are some types of financing not being done in the area? Is there a reason behind it? For example, if few lower-priced homes are subject to FHA financing, it might be an indication that the properties are in disrepair or physically unable to meet FHA appraisal specifications (due to water quality, septic problems, etc.). If certain types of financing are not available, that could slow down your marketing time when you resell.

3. Where is the neighborhood in the real estate cycle? Is it progressing or regressing? Real estate analysts will tell you that all neighborhoods go through cycles, typically about every 10 to 15 years, somewhat like generations. Which side of the cycle is the neighborhood on?

For example, you can probably pay less if you purchase a home when the neighborhood is at the low end of the cycle, but you're also going to have less appreciation and perhaps have problems reselling if properties around yours deteriorate.

A prime example of this was the Farmers Home Administration subsidized housing boom of the mid-1970s. I can remember selling new houses for $18,000 in vast subdivisions of one-acre lots. The problem was that most people who could only afford to purchase a house with government-subsidized funds couldn't afford the upkeep and maintenance involved. Many of the homes became ill kept, a wasteland for junker cars, and foreclosures skyrocketed. This was the bottom of the cycle. Even the owners who had properly maintained their homes had trouble selling due to the surrounding environment.

But the good news was that once new owners purchased the foreclosed properties and the real estate market heated up (causing fewer homes to be on the market), values increased and the neighborhood was once again looking up.

If you're going to be reselling the property in the not-too-distant future, you can see why careful evaluation of neighborhood and real estate trends is vital.

4. Check information sources to determine trends. You can check the assessed value from the county assessor to determine if values are swinging up or dipping down. Other external forces can have impact, too, such as commercial development closing in on an area or property being condemned by the government to build roads or parks.

Decide If Buying the Most Unusual Home in the Neighborhood Makes Sense

You've undoubtedly heard real estate investors say, "Buy on the low side of the market so you'll have room to improve the property." There's merit to that advice. That's why you need to see how the property you're considering "fits" in the neighborhood. Is it currently at the high end, the low end, or somewhere in the middle? All things considered, if you can buy the home that is similar in square footage to others in the neighborhood, but doesn't have all of the bells, buzzers, and whistles of the other houses, you're on the safe side. You should have room to make cost-effective improvements, add to your equity by doing so, and be able to get your money out when you sell.

But what about the unique property in the neighborhood? Since nearly everyone covets that one, why wouldn't it be a good buy? Answer: For all the reasons we've mentioned previously!

First, getting the appraisal you need on a specialty home may be tough since there are few (if any) comps. (And this could equally be true when you resell.)

Second, the lender may be cautious because a specialty home may be on the high side of the market, may take longer to sell (in the case of default), and may require another specialty buyer to purchase it again. It's just more risk to the lender, as well as the private mortgage insurer who insures the lender against the borrower's default.

If you do take the plunge and purchase the one-of-a-kind house, do it with a game plan in mind. Be willing to hold it until the rest of the neighborhood catches up, know that reselling may take longer, and generally polish up that crystal ball to anticipate the future!

Evaluate Whether Buying a House That "Needs Changes" Is in Your Best Interest

With many buyers qualifying for less loan and less house than in the past, there's a common refrain among buyers: "Even though this house is not exactly what we want, we can always improve it after we're in." Maybe yes, maybe no.

I'm not trying to be a wet blanket here, but you should be aware that there are some things that you *can* change (physically and financially) and others that an act of Congress won't change!

Here's a scenario to prove the point. Mark and Mattie Moskowitz buy a house that's much smaller than what they had in mind, but they like the neighborhood (which is full of other two-bedroom homes) and figure they can always add a third bedroom before they start their family.

Six months after closing, they secure a loan to add on to the house. When the contractor tries to secure the building permits, he learns that there's inadequate space to add the bedroom and still have the necessary set-back from the rear lot line. There's no where else to put the bedroom. Mark and Mattie Moskowitz have just purchased a house that can't be expanded, and they'll lose money now if they sell.

The moral? Check out the expansion possibilities before purchasing. And be aware that if you do make major improvements, you run the risk of overimproving the property for the neighborhood. (Probably not in Mark and Mattie's case since values in the neighborhood were sound.)

In Step #10 of the Homebuying Game, we'll give you tips to "Manage Your Castle," including types of home improvements that do add dollars to your equity and others that you should avoid if you expect to get money back when you sell. If you have particular questions about improving the property you're considering, turn to Step #10 right now to look for specific answers to your questions.

If you've met the ten challenges of "Choose the Best House," then congratulations, IT'S YOUR MOVE to Homebuying Step #7 ♨

If you've faltered on any of the steps, then GO TO THE PENALTY BOX.

Penalty Box

Possible penalties could include the following:

1. Purchasing property that loses its value and subsequently costs you money when you sell (because you failed to purchase in the best neighborhood you could afford)
2. Living an uncomfortable lifestyle in a home that's "not you" because you failed to weigh the pros and cons
3. Experiencing sleepless nights worrying about crime and property damage since you failed to check out the safety of the neighborhood

For "help" out of the PENALTY BOX:

1. Walk around, check around, and ask around the neighborhood before you get "serious" about the house.
2. Prioritize the home's features so that when you find your dream home, you'll know it!
3. Know that you'll have an advantage in going with both a home inspection and a home warranty for your property.

 Take Trump Card #6

Nothing is more important than taking the necessary time to check out the neighborhood, the property, and the lifestyle you'll be taking on when you buy a home. Protect your family, protect your pocketbook, and protect your peace of mind by choosing the best property to meet your needs.

Step 7

Sharpen Your Pencil

Negotiate the Best Price and Terms

You've found the house you want and you've physically checked it out (as well as the surrounding area), so your next step is to buy it. Keep in mind the adage we quoted earlier: "You make money on real estate when you *buy* it, not when you sell it." So sharpen that pencil and make money with your purchase!

No other phase of the real estate purchase better exemplifies the term *game* than does negotiating the purchase. The seller wants the most he can get; you want to pay the least. The seller doesn't want to part with precious equity to pay for anything that's not customarily his cost of sale; you may be hard-pressed to come up with an ample down payment and money for closing costs. Two sets of players on opposite sides of the same coin, trying to win at the same game!

That's why buyers and sellers need to understand certain immutable rules that govern real estate negotiating. Stick to the rules and you win the game; attempt to defy the rules and you'll lose out (or at least make yourself crazy *trying* to win it all!).

You may be inclined to think that a checklist of sharp-shooter, slam dunk strategies will follow. Not so. These tips are based on common sense and an honest approach to helping both parties get what they want.

If you're working with the assistance of a real estate agent, you may not have to apply these negotiating strategies directly— but you will be a part of the process.

The Rules for Negotiating a Win/Win Purchase

1. Try to determine the other party's hot buttons and address them in your offer. If the seller has been relocated and has to be at her new job in three weeks, speak to a quick closing. If the seller needs a full price offer to clear debts in order to sell, pay your own closing costs and ask for no contributions from the seller. Contrary to popular belief, getting her price may not be the seller's sole or even paramount motive. Other hot buttons may be equally, or perhaps more, important.

2. Always place yourself emotionally in the other party's shoes before making an offer. Try to understand his or her position. Information may be power, but empathy goes just as far when you're negotiating for a win/win outcome.

3. The first offer sets the stage for what's to come. Your initial negotiating pattern can dictate how the balance of the negotiations will play out. If you make an incredibly low or even insulting offer, you may receive the same treatment from the seller (or no response at all). If you nickel-and-dime the seller, expect to be nickel-and-dimed back!

4. Never have just one last issue to negotiate, because someone will win; someone will lose. No one wants to lose— especially if it's you!

5. Bottom line: You may expect to win all the marbles, but it won't happen! Decide what's most important for you to win; then decide which of *those* marbles you're willing to part with if you have to. It's all give and take.

Now that you've got an overview of the rules, let's review each in depth. So IT'S YOUR MOVE ⬥

Determine the Seller's Hot Buttons

If you have kids, you probably can relate to this vignette. My daughter Crystal came to me when she first started junior high school, asking if she could take skiing lessons. While she was a good athlete, her request was curious since she hated being out in the cold (a slight roadblock growing up in Idaho). I said she could take the lessons, but didn't uncover her true motivating hot button until classes started several weeks later. A young man that Crystal had her eye on lived at the end of the street and was taking the very same lessons and riding the very same bus to the ski lift. Now it all made sense.

Similarly, all sellers have hot buttons that serve as the underlying motivating factor(s). These could relate to why they are selling, their timetable for doing so, and what they hope to accomplish by selling. Hot buttons are the most important goal the seller wants to achieve or the item the seller wants to win. And sometimes, the seller won't even admit the hot buttons to himself or herself—but after reviewing the facts, you and/or your agent may be able to sort them out to help get the seller to "yes."

Now that you know how important it is to address the seller's hot buttons whenever possible, IT'S YOUR MOVE ♠

Decide If You Should Make a Full-Price Offer

Besides asking the obvious question of whether the property is worth a full-price offer, check out whether getting a full-price offer is a must for this seller. Some sellers insist on getting their price because they have large outstanding mortgages to pay off, or they need all they can get to put down on another house—the financial reasons can be endless (and perhaps justified if the house is properly priced).

But sometimes you'll run across a seller who "has to get her price" for purely emotional reasons. For example, she overpaid for the house when she bought it and is now trying to save face when she sells; or a next-door neighbor "got his price" so she wants to as well.

No matter what the seller's motive, the listed or asking price can be a major (albeit distorted) factor in the mind of the seller. Here's why.

Many sellers don't think in terms of what they'll net from the sale (the amount of the check they receive at closing), only the *price* they receive. And the two aren't necessarily the same. In fact, it's possible for a seller to net more at closing from a lower-price than a full-price offer. This is because the full-price offer might require the seller to pay more closing costs, points, and work repairs. So even though the offered price was less, the seller's bottom line might even be more than with a full-price offer! (Later in this Step, we'll explain how a seller's net sheet can determine what the seller will "net" from the sale.)

 If you determine that it's not so important to offer this particular seller's full price, be prepared to offer a trade-off reward of equal or near-equal value.

After it's been determined the importance of a full-price offer to the seller, IT'S YOUR MOVE ♣

 ## Place Yourself Emotionally in the Seller's Shoes

It's been said that true negotiating power lies in gaining the emotional support of the other party. In other words, if the seller can understand where you're coming from, he can empathize with the logical requests you make.

Just as we explored the emotional side of homebuying, you merely have to flip the coin to see what sellers go through emotionally. For some sellers, their home is a legacy of family history with fond memories of birthday parties, evenings by the fire, and joyous family holidays of years past.

For other sellers, the house might merely be one of several houses in a series of locations, seen more as a financial investment than a mainstay in their life. It just depends on the sellers.

Nevertheless, if you try to place yourself in their shoes emotionally, your offers will be more fair and you will be more willing to compromise if need be to create a win/win situation.

Now that we're empathizing with the seller, IT'S YOUR MOVE ♣

Design Your First Offer to Set the Stage for Future Negotiations

This simple negotiating principle is one area where many buyers lose ground, never to regain it. Your first offer sets the negotiating pattern, good or bad. This can often lead to not getting the property since the other party may be insulted and unwilling to negotiate further.

Here's an example. The Craners want the house, but think they'll "lowball it" to see just how low the sellers might go.

Upon seeing an offer $10,000 less than their asking price, the Harps are infuriated, and counter back to the buyers at $1,000 *over* their original listing price.

Back and forth the negotiations go, neither side willing to give the other an inch. In the end, pride (and foolish first negotiations) end up losing the house for the buyers and the sale for the sellers.

You'll often see negotiations like this start out in incremental patterns. For example, the buyer and seller might be $3,000 apart, then $1,500, then $750 (meeting each other halfway as they go). The problem is that if a party balks at going further, someone wins, someone loses, or the sale may fall apart all together.

A buyer or seller could tire of negotiating and give up. Some people love the challenge of the game and have a heart for it; others just want it to be over. Just as in financing the sale, if negotiations drag on too long, the risk is much higher that the sale will never be consummated.

If you understand that first offers set the stage for negotiations to come, IT'S YOUR MOVE ✦

 Have More Than One Issue to Negotiate

Let's say that you've decided three things are worth negotiating: price, the closing date, and having the seller pay two discount points.

You win on the price; the closing date is flexible; but try as you might, you just can't sway the seller to pay those two discount points. Why? It is the last issue to negotiate, and given that the seller had already conceded on the first two items, there is no earthly way you are going to win the third too!

That's why it's wise never to have just one item remaining to negotiate—someone will win, someone will lose. It would have been much better to throw in a bogus item that you really didn't care much about in order to win the discount points. By letting the other party win on one of the two points, your success rate would have climbed.

Keeping in mind that having just one final issue can be dangerous to your negotiating position, IT'S YOUR MOVE

Know What You Want to Win and What You're Willing to Give Up

As mentioned earlier, know what's most important for you to win and what you're willing to give up to get it! If a lowered purchase price is what you're aiming for, what are you willing to give the seller? A quick closing? Allowing the seller to rent back for a time after closing? The idea is to decide what's of little value to you and trade it for something of greater value to the seller.

The bottom line is that in win/win negotiating, no one gets all the marbles. Decide what's most important to you and try to hold out for it. But don't forget other major factors that come into play. These include whether the market is a buyer's or a seller's market, the number of properties available, and how fast properties are selling. All the negotiating strategies in the world won't make up for a shortage of property.

If there's a shortage of property, decide what you're willing to do, and then do it—quick! When we purchased a second home in Idaho, I was amazed when our buyer's agent told us that if we really wanted the house, we should make a cash offer with a quick closing and no contingencies. I reminded her that I always negotiate, try not to use too much of my own cash, and, of course, wanted to make the purchase contingent upon getting a loan.

She asked if we really wanted the house. I said, "Yes, of course." She said (and I quote), "If you mess around negotiating, you'll lose this house. Once this property comes on the open market, there will be multiple cash offers. If you take this risk, I won't be responsible for the outcome!"

We did what she said and got the house. Two weeks after closing we moved some furniture to the house, only to find various notes (and even an earnest money check!) in the door from passersby who thought the house was empty and potentially for sale. I am convinced that had we dallied trying to win various negotiating battles, we would have lost the war. (This also taught me that while I know real estate, it's certainly worth working with an expert in the local market if you want to come out ahead.)

Once you've prioritized what's most important for you to win as well as what you're willing to leave on the table, IT'S YOUR MOVE ✦

 ## Be Aware of Negotiating Strategies That Might Occur

While we hope the seller you encounter works toward win/win negotiating, there can always be the exception—sellers who want to get all of the marbles for themselves!

If you run into this type, be prepared to weather various negotiating gambits. These could include the following:

Budget limitations.   Variations on this theme include, "We can't go any lower because we need that much money for our new house," or "I refuse to pay for any of the buyer's costs—what do I look like, the bank?"

Antidote: Remember that it's not necessarily price but net proceeds that the seller should focus on. Second, the seller should be reminded that everything is give and take—if he wants you to "give" him his price, he'll have to "take" money from his proceeds to help with your closing costs!

Nibbling/whittling.   This technique is generally used once negotiations are finalized (although this gambit can occur within the body of the negotiations too). The seller might tell your agent, "No, I never said I would leave the microwave. If the buyer wants it, he can give me cash for it." "Of course the drapery rods don't stay—we paid a premium for those." The seller is "nibbling away" at what has already been negotiated.

Antidote: Make sure everything is spelled out in writing; and if you do amend the agreement, make sure all parties to the sale initial and date all changes.

Good guy/bad buy.   This gambit occurs when the sellers want to buy time before making a decision and/or want to sway or counter the direction of the sale. One of them is the good guy, the other the bad guy. They are very rarely in the same room or location together, as this can lessen their impact as a team. For example, the husband might say to your real estate agent, "I don't know if my wife would part with the antique table. She's pretty attached to it. I'll ask her and get back to you." He'd later call his agent back to announce, "Tell the buyer's agent that my wife won't include the table in the sale but would take $200 extra for it." He's the good guy for asking; she is the powerful one at a distance making the decision—but they both win.

Antidote: If both you and the seller are working through real estate agents, this is a tough one to orchestrate since you'll have no control over how and when the offer is presented to the sellers. But if you're working directly with the sellers, make sure both parties are together for all negotiations. Ask if their joint consensus is needed to make the final decision or if one can speak for both parties. Have both sign and acknowledge all paperwork.

Higher authority.   One or both of the players must defer to a third party for answers and/or approval. This could be a lender, an appraiser, a relative, even a boss. It's one way to stall for time and to evaluate all options before committing.

Antidote: Set short time frames for responding to you and communicate to the seller that you know he/she is capable of making sound decisions, with or without third-party input. (You'll very quickly find out if the higher authority is necessary to the decision-making process. If so, then consider that it's a roadblock and time frame that you'll have to deal with.)

The stall.   The stall is a decision not to make a decision. It usually shows that while the seller has some positive thoughts on the offer, there are also some negative points that need to be addressed. In real estate, it could also signal that the seller is anticipating receiving another offer and wants to buy time until it materializes.

Antidote: Your agent will ask the listing agent to isolate the seller's individual concerns about the offer, asking questions like, "What could we change that would convince you to take this offer now?" While you need to build the seller's desire to accept the offer now, don't forget that you have a powerful negotiating tool you can use here as well—revoking the offer before it is accepted by the seller. (We'll cover the basics of withdrawing offers later in this Step.) While this may seem like a dire measure, there's no harm in communicating to the seller that you know you can withdraw the offer at any time before receiving the seller's signed acceptance." This may be just the nudge the seller requires to make a decision.

"Reduce it to the ridiculous."   This really is an effective tactic. The idea is to make something you're negotiating for seem so insignificant that the other party would appear a fool to say no! For example, the seller might say, "Tell that buyer that the extra $5,000 in price is just 85¢ a day over the life of the loan! Surely that little amount wouldn't stand in the way of them buying this house!" (See how effective that is.)

Antidote: Expand the item back to its full size . . . and then some. Your response communicated to the seller could be, "Tell him that the $5,000 financed over the life of the loan, including interest, actually makes it $13,308! And that makes this house *way too expensive*!" (I rest my case.)

Once you're aware that these negotiating gambits may occur, then IT'S YOUR MOVE ⤬

 ## Structure Your Offer with Power

Picture yourself as a seller comparing two offers on your property. One is vague, containing merely the basics of price and the amount of earnest money offered. And while the second offer is for the same price, it itemizes the costs that both seller and buyer will pay, the type of financing the buyer will obtain—even the time frame for doing so. Which offer would you feel more comfortable choosing? Of course, the more detailed one.

Keep this analogy in mind when you and/or you and the real estate agent write up your offer to the seller. If you're vague on some points or fail to address them at all, you may create red flags in the seller's mind. And by remaining silent on certain issues, you could be opening them up for interpretation later. Be as complete as you can in spelling out what will happen and who will pay for which costs. It should result in a much smoother transaction.

Give Your First Offer "Your Best Shot"

You may have heard buyers claim to their agent, "Let's start with a low offer to the seller. We can always come up later." Contrary to popular belief, at times this thinking is faulty and the buyer loses in the end.

Here's why. An unrealistically low price could insult the seller, causing the seller to make a weak counteroffer or, worse yet, no counteroffer at all! Remember what we said about the first offer setting the stage for future negotiations? A low initial offer is a prime case in point. The seller may be angered and decide to withhold any concessions he was thinking of making. Since the selling process first affects the seller on an emotional level, an unrealistically low offer can serve as a slap in the face to some sellers.

If you decide that making a low initial offer won't do too much damage, there's one last consideration before you act. While you're making low offers, the seller might decide to take another offer, particularly if yours appears to be way off the mark. The seller may conclude, "Well, if this buyer really wanted the property, why did he waste time with this ridiculous offer?" The bottom line: It's good to have a strategy for making offers, but remember that testing the water with low offers might be wasting precious time that could end up costing you the property!

How Much Earnest Money Should You Offer?

A substantial earnest money deposit not only shows that you're acting in good faith, but also intimates that you have the financial wherewithal to purchase the property. That's why it's one of the areas where you can show power in your negotiations and add teeth to an otherwise weak offer.

Here's a technique I learned as a real estate broker from a buyer in the early 1980s. I call it "cash talks." With prices flat and the buyer pressing me to present his less-than-full-price offer to the seller of a small rental house, the buyer knew he needed an ace in the hole. So he reached in his bib overalls and pulled out 20 crisp one-hundred-dollar bills (substantial earnest money for the purchase price he was offering). "Here," he said, "show *these* to the seller!" I obeyed. Upon seeing the money and the offer, the seller replied, "Well, I guess he *does* have money. Let's take his offer. Oh, and by the way, can I keep that cash?" Unfortunately, it had to be initially deposited in our brokerage trust account, but

I was able to release part of it to the seller once I got him and the buyer to agree to it in writing. The buyer's strategy had worked. The substantial deposit sent the perception (erroneous or not) to the seller that there was more money where that came from!

There is no standard in the real estate industry that dictates how much earnest money you should offer. One real estate agent might tell you 10 percent of the purchase price is good; another agent might suggest 1 percent. In fact, you could even offer the seller a promissory note (a promise to pay) to be converted to cash after the seller accepts the offer. (Note that this is not a strong way to present an offer. The seller might question if the promissory note would ever be converted to cash as well as worry about the time it would take to make the conversion.) Whatever you decide, remember that more is usually better than less. And be prepared to suffer the consequences of losing a property to another buyer if your offer is up against an identical one that offers more earnest money. Earnest money does talk and sellers do listen.

State the Time Frame for the Seller's Acceptance

A major tool of sound negotiation is to set a reasonable time frame for the seller's acceptance of your offer. But the key is to consider the seller's circumstances as well as the circumstances surrounding the sale of the property.

For example, if you specify that the seller has 48 hours to accept the offer, but it turns out that the seller is on a cruise to the Bahamas, the time frame for acceptance has been too short. Contrarily, if you specify that the seller has seven days to accept or reject the offer, you may be opening yourself up for competing offers that could cost you the property or drive up the asking price. If the property is one of a kind and it's a seller's market, you may be wise to use a short time frame to respond so that the seller will be motivated to make a quick decision about your offer.

The key: Gauge the response time the seller has to accept your offer based on the individual circumstances of that seller and the property. In general (unless there's information that would dictate something to the contrary), shorter deadlines are better than longer. Most sellers who are truly interested in responding to your offer will either do so as soon as possible or ask for an extension of the deadline. From your standpoint, a short time frame shows that you are interested in getting an answer and assumes that the seller is equally interested in providing one. The real estate agent you're working with will be able to give you an idea of the customary time frames used in the area and help you decide if this situation warrants a longer time frame.

Later in this Step, we'll cover the subject of counteroffers. This will give you a good idea of why a seller should move quickly to accept or reject your offer because until the offer is bilaterally accepted by the parties, there is a chance it can be revoked by the offeror (which is you if you're making the offer to the seller).

Contingencies You May Want in Your Offer

Most preprinted purchase agreements (like the ones real estate agents use) address the most common contingencies for your purchase. But if you're a Lone Wolf, this is one of the areas where assistance by a real estate agent and/or a real estate attorney is well worth the time and cost. Let's review the most common contingencies and then add several others that may benefit you.

Financing contingencies.   This clause states that your offer is contingent upon receiving approval to obtain a certain type and amount of financing, by a certain date, with costs not to exceed a certain amount. Here's an example: "This offer is contingent upon the buyer applying for (within five business days) and receiving approval to receive a 90 percent conventional 30-year fixed rate loan with interest not to exceed 9 percent and discount points not to exceed 2 percent of said loan amount." (In a preprinted form, blank spaces are usually provided to fill in the amounts that apply.) You could add more specifics if you consider it important. The idea is to acquire a reasonable period of time to obtain financing and to bail out of the sale (with your earnest money being returned) if financing isn't available.

Appraisal contingencies.   This clause is used in a majority of purchase agreements, especially in sales where financing is required. Most lenders will make mortgage approval contingent on receiving an appraisal for at least the amount of the purchase agreement.

Home inspection contingencies. This has become a staple of most purchase agreements in the past few years. Be sure to read this clause carefully, as it may contain limits to which the seller agrees to repair the property, either as a certain percentage of the sale price or as a maximum dollar amount. Depending on the circumstances, you may want to consider striking seller financial caps here (or add financial caps that would apply to you) to prevent your being stuck with excessive repair costs that the lender might require for loan approval.

Insurance/flood insurance contingencies. Since Hurricane Andrew ripped through South Florida, causing havoc among insurance companies, real estate agents can be heard telling homebuyers, "Get your homeowners insurance and then we'll find the house!" Remarkably, this statement is not far from the truth and it reminds the buyer to check both the general insurability of the property as well as any special insurance needs required (flood, hurricane, tornado, earthquake) before making an offer. As a buyer, make sure that you list the type of insurance needed as a contingency in the offer to purchase.

Other special contingencies. You'll need to add the following items to most purchase agreements:

- Obtaining the down payment: If your down payment is coming from a relative, an employer, or other outside source, make sure that you make the offer contingent upon receiving these funds by a certain date.
- Other endorsers: If someone else is needed for cosigning, approving the property (like a relative giving you a gift letter), or serving as a coborrower, make your offer contingent upon receiving that assistance by a certain date.
- Other situations that must first happen: If you're waiting for your existing home to sell and close, a zoning change to occur on the property, or the seller to complete a repair on the home, your offer could reflect the contingency.

You can see that while contingencies help you buy time in the purchase, they can also be a detriment if the seller has the choice between your offer with contingencies and one without. Use contingencies only when necessary. Too many can weaken your offer and throw up red flags to the seller that you may not be a strong buyer or someone who's not ready to buy at this time.

Now that you've decided which clauses and contingencies you should use in your offer, IT'S YOUR MOVE ♣

 ## Sell Your Offer to the Seller

Remember what we said previously about the power of using a third-party negotiator to advocate your position? If you've been working without the benefit of a real estate agent up to this point, you could still enlist one to negotiate for you now. It could help separate you from the emotional issues of negotiating for something you have fallen for and want to own and should make your offer come from more of a business position than from an emotional one.

Additionally, you may need help preparing a net sheet for the seller (note the information that follows). This is a critical point of power in getting the seller to accept your offer.

Use a Seller's Net Sheet to Help Your Position

The seller's net sheet shows exactly what your offer will cost in financial terms and approximately how much the seller will "net" at closing. (See Figure 7.1.) This is a powerful negotiating tool, because many sellers focus heavily on getting "their price" and are unaware that there can be a big difference between price and "net."

Keep this premise in mind when you're determining how to structure your offer to the seller—an offer with a lower offered price could actually net more cash to a seller at closing.

Here's an example. Let's say you have a choice of two different types of loans—a Veterans Administration loan (VA) at 8.5 percent with two discount points (2 percent of the loan amount) or a conventional loan at 8.25 percent with no points. The seller has not mentioned whether she's willing to pay discount points, as points are negotiable. But you're interested in getting the lowest interest rate you can and the lowest possible monthly payment, so you make the following offer.

You offer her a price of $85,000 ($1,000 less than her listed price) *but* you go with the conventional loan so no points are involved. The offer is *sold* to her by the agent, who states, "Had

FIGURE 7.1   Seller's Estimation Sheet

Prepared for _____   Address _____

Prepared by _____   Estimated Closing Date _____

Selling Price .... $ _____

Approximate Indebtedness

    First Loan .... @ _____ % $ _____

    Second Loan .... @ _____ % $ _____

    Other .... @ _____ % $ _____

Gross Equity .... $ _____

Seller's Estimated Costs:

    Brokerage Fee .... $ _____

    Title Insurance Policy (Sales Price) .... $ _____

    Long-Term Escrow Set-Up Fee .... $ _____

    Escrow Closing Fee .... $ _____

    Mortgage Discount .... $ _____

    Contract Preparation .... $ _____

    Attorney Fees .... $ _____

    Appraisal Fee .... $ _____

    Interest to Closing .... $ _____

    Property Tax Proration .... $ _____

    Payoff Penalty .... $ _____

    Recording Fees .... $ _____

    Reconveyance Fee .... $ _____

    Required Repairs .... $ _____

    City Inspection .... $ _____

    Local Improvement Districts (LIDs) Assessment .... $ _____

    Misc. .... $ _____

    _____ .... $ _____

If Income Property:

    Prorated Rents .... $ _____

    Security or Cleaning Deposits .... $ _____

Less Total Estimated Costs .... $ _____

Subtotal .... $ _____

Estimated Credits

    Reserve Account .... $ _____

    _____ .... $ _____

Plus Total Credits .... $ _____

Estimated Seller's Proceeds .... $ _____

Less Loan Carried by Seller .... $ _____

Estimated Net Cash Proceeds .... $ _____

Seller _____   Date _____

the buyer taken a VA loan, he would have asked that you pay $1,720 in discount points ($86,000 × 2 percent on a zero-down-payment VA loan). By offering you $1,000 less on your price and waiving payment of the points, you will actually net $720 more than you would have with the other type of financing."

This scenario assumes that all the other costs between the two loans are equal, and it also assumes that the seller was willing to consider VA financing. However, you get the point: depending on the costs involved, a lower purchase price can often mean more money to the seller at closing. Your agent can help you structure your offer and use the net sheet provided to pencil out the savings.

Use Comps to Justify Your Offer

Here's where doing your homework in advance can help you reap great benefits! Use information you found about comparable properties (houses that are similar in style, in the same or similar neighborhoods, that have sold recently) to justify to the seller why you're making this offer. Information is power. There's no stronger way to convince a seller that he's high or that getting all cash for the house is not plausible than to use information about previous sales.

If a buyer's agent is representing you, she has more than likely done a comparative market analysis (CMA) on the property you're interested in. Similar to the CMA done for the seller by the listing agent, this is a powerful tool in convincing the seller that you've done your homework and know what the property should sell for.

Use Personal Property as a Negotiating Tool

Personal property used as a negotiating tool—it can be the biggest nightmare or a negotiator's dream. It all depends on how and when it's used.

The seller has mentioned that although it won't be part of the purchase price, the refrigerator could be purchased separately. How could you use that information when making your offer? You could include the refrigerator as part of a full-price offer. You could include the refrigerator (giving the seller nothing for it), stating that you didn't think the seller would want to move the refrigerator. In other words, the refrigerator becomes a positive piece of negotiating fodder.

However, using personal property as leverage can backfire at times. Here's an example. You include the refrigerator in your initial $3,000 less-than-listed price offer to the seller.

The seller counters at full price and states that you *can't* have the refrigerator.

You counter to him, increasing your offered price by $1,000 and asking once again for the refrigerator.

The seller counters at full price once again (asking you to increase your offer by another $2,000), but this time, he gives you the refrigerator. You agree and sign the offer.

What happened here? It's difficult to know the true role the refrigerator played in this negotiation. But that $300 refrigerator might have just cost you $3,000! You as the buyer got so caught up in winning all of the marbles that you failed to see that one of the marbles certainly wasn't worth a $3,000 loss! The moral: evaluate the true cost of the item you're bartering for and make sure that winning it at all cost doesn't become literal!

Sometimes sellers become emotionally attached to personal property and can therefore place a much higher value on it than it's worth. If you keep this in mind in negotiating personal property, you'll be able to keep a clear head about what you may be able to win and what may be an exercise in futility!

One last point. If and when you do negotiate personal property as part of the transaction, it's wise to identify it as succinctly as you can, down to the serial number, if possible. Why? There are sellers who want to get "one last marble." So they try the old "switcho-chango" on personal property, as the scenario demonstrates.

As a real estate broker, I once had a buyer who negotiated aggressively to get the seller to leave the GE side-by-side refrigerator with the house. Well, the seller *did* leave a GE refrigerator—a circa 1940 model worth about 42 cents. And, unfortunately, I made no mention of the refrigerator's age, style, model, or serial number on either the listing agreement or the purchase agreement, only that it was a GE refrigerator. You only have to buy *one* side-by-side refrigerator for a buyer to get smart about details in a real estate transaction!

Yes, the seller still might have "appropriated" the refrigerator as they moved out. But had I been more definitive with the paperwork (especially the purchase agreement), *he* probably would have been paying for that refrigerator, not me!

Selling Trade-Offs to the Seller

Real estate negotiations are all give and take. So be prepared to show the seller *where* you have given and what you're asking in return.

If you've offered the seller's full price, that can be justification for requesting that he pay discount points.

If you're offering a lower price, you can do some offsetting with a hefty earnest money deposit.

If you're asking the seller to pay a majority of the closing costs, you'd better be prepared to show how you've compensated for it with other concessions.

And don't assume that the seller will be able to see the concessions you're making. You or your agent needs to point them out to the seller and/or his agent and discuss your rationale for being fair. This helps the seller feel that you really do want the purchase to come together and are willing to make concessions to make it happen.

You've written the offer, now it's showtime!

Presenting Your Offer—How It Works

Your offer can be presented in numerous ways. Your real estate agent, if you have one, may have an approach for presenting your offer. But if you're "going it alone" as a Lone Wolf, the steps that follow may be helpful.

1. Call in advance for an appointment to meet with the seller. (It's good to have someone other than yourself make the call—that way the seller won't be tempted to ask leading questions like "Is it a full-price offer?" If that happens, the person calling can honestly say, "I don't know.")
2. Begin your discussion of the offer with the positives involved (e.g., quick closing, full price, seller keeps the refrigerator and stove, etc.) Your intent is to build strong,

positive momentum that can help offset any negatives you'll be presenting.

3. Next present the net sheet, particularly if you're not offering full price. This can assure the seller that his net cash will not be too much less than he had anticipated (especially if you structure the offer with trade-offs in mind—we discuss this later in the Step.)

4. Follow the net sheet with the formal offer. Again focus on the positives and let the seller read the offer to pick up any negatives. (This is not meant to be deceiving. You are working to "sell" the offer to the seller by emphasizing the positive aspects and playing down the negative ones.) Be honest with the seller when asked about any negative aspects of the offer.

5. Be prepared to show supporting material about why you offered what you did (i.e., comparable property information, estimates on what repairs will cost, etc.)

6. Ask if the seller is prepared to give you a decision now. If not, inform the seller about the time frame for acceptance you've stated on the offer and ask him to contact you at or before that time.

7. It's good to remind the seller that real estate contract law allows you (the offeror) to revoke the offer any time before its acceptance is communicated to you from the seller (the offeree). This lets the seller know that a timely decision is in his best interest as well as yours.

8. Never be confrontational with the seller. If things begin to get heated, ask the seller when it would be convenient to call back for a response to the offer. Since much of what the seller first feels is emotional, tempers can flare. Put yourself in the seller's shoes and act accordingly.

9. Be prepared to walk away. True negotiating power lies in the ability to keep your "walk away" option open.

Now that you've presented your offer, IT'S YOUR MOVE

 ## Win with Counteroffers

You've presented your offer to the seller. And while she doesn't seem to object to most provisions of the offer, there are things she wants to change. Her offer back to you on these changes then becomes a second offer, also known as a counteroffer.

What is a counteroffer and how is it created? Technically, it's an entirely new offer and is created when either you or the seller changes one or more items on the purchase agreement or you write up an entirely new offer. That's why the counteroffer is so powerful: it is an entirely new agreement that doesn't have to be accepted by the other party.

For example, let's say that the seller looks at your offer and says she agrees with everything except leaving the stove. She scratches through the mention of the stove in the personal property section of the offer, initials the contract and hands it across the table to you. Her alteration of that original offer has created a whole new offer—one that *you* don't have to accept. So if you disagree with the alteration, in essence the seller has just thrown the sale of her $100,000 home for the price of a $200 stove! Now you see why the counteroffer can be a power tool when negotiating. (And it doesn't hurt to remind the seller that by making even minor changes to the agreement, it becomes technically an entirely new offer that you don't have to agree to!)

The first counteroffer sets the stage for future negotiations.
Just as your first negotiations set a pattern, so does your first counteroffer. For example, if you and the seller are $5,000 apart in price and you come up $2,500 (so that you're now $2,500 apart), it may indicate to the seller that she should come up with the equal $2,500. Be willing to give an equal increment to what you expect to receive and be prepared to point this out to the seller.

One caution that we've mentioned previously: never have just one item to negotiate, especially where price is concerned. Let's say that counteroffers back and forth between you and the seller are in increments of $100. What happens when you get to the final $100? Someone will win and someone will lose. No one wants to be the last one to give in. The solution? Always have two trade-offs working at all times. Then you can win on the $100 increment and let the seller win to keep that darn stove!

If your offer isn't first in line—the backup offer. What if you come across the property of your dreams late in the game and there's already an offer on it? Is there anything you can do? Perhaps. You could make an offer, and, if accepted by the seller, it could become a backup offer to the one currently in first position on the property. Why would a seller do this? So that he would have alternatives should the first offer fold.

But why would a buyer want to be in a backup position? If the property is a one-of-a kind house, the buyer is willing to wait to see if she could obtain it and especially if the first offer is subject to contingencies, the buyer might want to stand pat.

But the downside is just that—unless you can afford to purchase both homes (should the first offer on this property fall), you probably shouldn't be making offers on others. One alternative: You can stipulate in your offer that you reserve the right to revoke this offer before the seller places it in a first position if you find another suitable property.

You can see that backup offers are a game of roulette—and as is true of any other game, you should know what you stand to win or lose before you roll the dice. You can also see that this is yet another area where having the assistance of a real estate agent or a real estate attorney will definitely increase your odds of drafting paperwork that accomplishes what you need it to.

Now that you've mastered offers and counteroffers, IT'S YOUR MOVE ♣

 ## What to Do When the Seller Says "No"

You've presented your offer to the seller. She is not impressed, nor does she give you any indication that she will come back to you with a second, or counter, offer. What can you do if the seller says "no"?

1. Determine if you feel the seller is reasonable in what you think she wants. For example, if you've known that the property was grossly overpriced all along and feel that the seller would sooner die in the house than be reasonable, you may want to concentrate your efforts on another seller

(especially if you're on a tight deadline to purchase and/ or numerous properties are available).

2. Analyze where the greatest roadblock lies. Is it price, terms, timing, or personal property you've asked for? Determine what concessions you're willing to make and how far you're willing to go. If possible, make a counter-offer that concedes the seller's hot button. If you feel you have time (and no offers from other buyers are pending), you may decide to whittle or nibble at the concessions one by one. On what one point are you most willing to concede? If that's not effective, try a second concession.

3. Put time on your side. If you think it's wise to wait and not counter to the seller for a while, waiting may be effective. This strategy may give the illusion that you're not going to give the seller the world and you're interested in other properties. In addition, it allows emotions to calm down a bit and may give the seller time to reflect that the offer isn't that bad after all. In fact, sometimes when the buyer backs away from the negotiations, the seller actually makes an offer back to the buyer! Wouldn't *that* be nice?

If you've conquered the 11 challenges of "Sharpen your Pencil," congratulations, IT'S YOUR MOVE to Step #8

But if you've fallen short negotiating the sale, then GO TO THE PENALTY BOX:

Penalty Box

Possible penalties include:

1. Losing your earnest money deposit by not writing the necessary contingencies into your offer
2. Losing a property you love because you failed to uncover and address the seller's hot buttons in your offer
3. Paying more than you need to because you failed to realize the seller was using negotiating gambits as leverage to win big

For "help" out of the PENALTY BOX:

1. Make a checklist of the important items that should go in your offer to purchase, including contingency clauses, time frames, and who will pay each closing cost.
2. Go back over what's important for you to win, as well as what you're willing to sacrifice to obtain the property.
3. Keep your emotions in check throughout the negotiating process. If possible, use a real estate agent to negotiate on your behalf.

 Take Trump Card #7

Knowledge is always power. Find out the most you can about the seller and his/her motivations and hot buttons *before* you structure and present your offer.

Step 8

Choose the Best Loan

STOP! If you've just turned to Step #8 and have not read Step #4, "Let the Lender Look in Your Wallet," you need to! The initial prequalifying interview as well as the loan application interview are far too important to take lightly. You may have found the ideal property and have good employment, but unless you can sail through the loan qualifying interview with the lender, there may not be a loan or a new home!

If you're still pulling information together for your appointment with the lender, see Figure 8.1. The explanation of its contents found in Step #4 will provide invaluable assistance.

Other Resources to Assist You

While it's impossible to cover a topic like financing in depth in this book, there are other resources, including a book I've written solely on that subject. It's called *All About Mortgages: Insider Tips to Finance the Home*, published by Dearborn Financial Publishing.

FIGURE 8.1   "Quick List" for Loan Application

1. Two years' residency information
2. Two years' employment information
3. Current pay stubs
4. If self-employed, two years' tax returns, and current profit and loss statement
5. Social Security number; age of borrower(s); number of years of school attended
6. Checking and savings accounts: account numbers and addresses
7. Information on monthly debt: account numbers, name, and location of creditor
8. Information on car loan(s): name and address of creditor
9. Lease and rental agreements
10. Copy of divorce decree
11. Information on child support, child care, alimony
12. Mortgages: account numbers and name and address of mortgagee
13. For FHA loans, driver's license(s) and Social Security cards
14. For VA loans, Certificate of Eligibility DD214

Chock full of checklists, comparison sheets, and market information, this easy-to-follow question and answer book will help make the mortgage process a breeze!

 Paying Cash versus Getting a Loan

This is the loan I vote for—none at all! No payments, no interest, no loan processing! Many of you may not be in a financial position to take this "nonoption" option, but some of you may be weighing paying cash versus getting a mortgage loan. That's right, there are negatives to paying cash!

Pros.   The benefits of paying cash for your home include the following:

1. Peace of mind that your property is free and clear of debt
2. No monthly payments and avoiding tens of thousands of dollars in interest

3. No time spent searching for and obtaining financing, and minimal closing costs
4. No property appraisal, as required with most mortgage loans
5. Take out a loan later and use the property as collateral, if desired
6. Leverage when making an offer and no contingencies typical with finance-required offers for either you or the seller

Cons.   The negatives of paying cash for your home include the following:

1. Depletes precious cash reserves, leaving you short for other major purchases and/or emergencies
2. Loss of tax advantages (If you borrow money later using consumer loans or credit cards, that's nondeductible interest.)
3. No appraisal as required by most lenders could be dangerous if the property is overpriced. (If inflation is low and/or you must sell in a short period of time, you might lose money on the property.)
4. Contrary to the first tenet of real estate leverage: Use OPM—other people's money—even if it is borrowed from the lender!
5. A required loan later would make you both the borrower and the seller for the purpose of paying closing costs.
6. If shopping for a mortgage later, the lender might consider the loan a refinance because you already own the property. (This could mean that you might not get as high a loan-to-value ratio as desired and/or the interest rate and fees might be higher.)

The bottom line on paying cash is to make sure you have ample cash reserves for emergencies (three to six months of your income), that you have a sound budget and financial game plan for your future (including ample insurance for catastrophes), and that you know how much leverage you could obtain should you later have to tap the property for cash.

Determine Which Mortgage Is Best for You

Most buyers do a great job of selecting the property and an okay job of selecting the lender, but when it comes to matching their financial needs with the best mortgage available, they often do an abysmal job that ends up costing them much more than it needs to! Why? Perhaps it's because the buyer has found his dream home and wants to move quickly to get it closed (settling for most any type of financing that comes along); or perhaps the borrower feels that, other than interest rates, most mortgages appear equal; or it could be that most buyers don't really know *how* to compare loans and choose the best one to meet their needs?

Consider this: How carefully would you shop for a car if you knew it had to (and could) last for the next 30 years? Probably pretty carefully. Yet many homebuyers are more cautious when it comes to buying a new car they'll keep for three years than they are shopping for hundred of thousands of dollars in funding for their family's home. Shopping for a mortgage is like shopping for any other major capital item—it has to be priced right, affordable, durable, usable, and able to last as long as needed.

That's why the first and most important guideline in choosing a loan is affordability: if you can't afford it over the long run, it won't work and may even end up costing you the property should you default!

Look for Long-Term Affordability in a Mortgage

Here is a loan affordability checklist to get you thinking in terms of the right loan for you:

1. What do you want to achieve by owning/financing this property? Do you want a quick equity buildup, an eventual nest egg to finance a child's college education? Will you hold the property only a short time? These answers will help you select the best loan to meet your needs, which is especially critical if you'll be selling the property in a short time.
2. How much of your savings do you want to use to fund the down payment and closing costs? This will help determine the size and type of loan.

3. How high a monthly payment are you prepared to make? You should gauge not only what the lender qualifies you for, but also what you're mentally prepared to make. These two amounts are often very different!

4. What are your current mortgage or rent payments? Lenders often use this as a benchmark, hesitant to approve new loans that are radically larger than the current payments unless a substantial income increase can be shown. (Lenders use the term *payment shock* to denote a borrower who undertakes a radically higher payment and finds he cannot make the payment, often leading to loan default.)

5. Would you mind if your payment amounts fluctuated (as they would with an adjustable rate mortgage)? If the answer is "yes," it may be best for you to steer clear of adjustable mortgage loan products even if you can save money by using one.

6. Will there be a coborrower (other than a spouse) on the loan? If so, you'll need to choose a loan that will allow coborrowers. The lender will direct you to products that will allow this.

Consider the Length of the Loan Term

Remember this tenet when choosing a mortgage: shorter is cheaper than longer!

When you compare the cost of a $100,000 30-year loan at 8 percent interest to that of a 15-year loan, the difference is more than $92,139 in additional payments!

So why wouldn't every buyer go with a shorter-term loan? Answer: the inability to qualify for the loan. First, the monthly principal and interest payment on the 15-year loan is $221.89 more than that for the 30-year loan ($955.66 compared with $733.77). And to qualify for that higher payment, a borrower using a conventional loan would need $793 more in monthly income. In today's world of downsizing and employment cutbacks, this may be impossible for many families.

In lieu of going with the higher payment, many borrowers choose to take the 30-year loan, hoping to reduce it by making prepayments. (We cover prepaying your loan in Step #10.) And yet other borrowers justify taking the longer-term loan, anticipating that they won't stay in the property long enough for extra payments to make the difference.

Finally, many lenders suggest that borrowers not burden themselves with the higher monthly payment when the lower one may help them accumulate savings or build some other investment vehicle. (But of course we know they have much to gain financially by suggesting this!)

If you're purchasing this home to retire in, you may want to consider a third option: a 10-year loan. While your payment in our $100,000 example will be $1,213.28, shaving five years off the 15-year loan will save you more than $26,000—a welcome boost to your retirement nest egg!

Evaluate what you can qualify for and compare that to how long you realistically will keep the loan on the property. This is the key to choosing the loan that will best suit your needs. The lender will be glad to show you cost projections to see which loan you qualify for (and are willing to make payments on) before you decide. See Figure 8.2 for a chart comparing various interest costs by loan term.

 ## Consider a Small versus a Large Down Payment

Sometimes, there is no choice—you have limited funds so it's a small down payment or no purchase at all!

But at other times, such as when you've just sold another home and you have money to spare, you need to consider whether using a small or a large down payment is best.

What are the pros and cons of using a small down payment when you purchase a home? The benefits are that you don't have all of your cash wrapped up in your home and can use it to create other investment opportunities. In addition, selling in a short period of time in an upswinging real estate market should allow you to pull your small down payment out in most cases (or at least break even when you sell).

However, in the case of a falling real estate market, using a very small down payment may mean that in order to sell quickly, you could find yourself in a deficit position, requiring you to bring your checkbook to closing! Ouch!

FIGURE 8.2   Comparing Interest Costs by Loan Term

The following table illustrates a $100,000 mortgage at 8.5% interest as paid to maturity under four different loan terms. Although the payment difference between the 30- and 15-year loans is $216, the interest saved over the term of the loan is $99,556!

Loan term	Monthly Payment	Months Paid	Total Cost	Total Interest Paid
30 years	$ 769	360	$276,809	$176,809
20 years	$ 868	240	$208,278	$108,278
15 years	$ 985	180	$177,253	$ 77,253
10 years	$1,240	120	$148,783	$ 48,783

Other reasons some buyers make sizable down payments (20 percent or more) are to sidestep paying private mortgage insurance on the loan and to take advantage of lower interest rates that may be available on low loan-to-value-ratio loans. And don't forget that a sizable down payment may also let the lender loosen some of the underwriting requirements on the loan. The key is to consider what you can afford as well as how long you'll own the property before deciding on the size of the down payment to make.

Discount Points and How They Work

A discount point, also called a *point,* is equal to 1 percent of the amount financed. If the lender tells you that the $75,000 loan you're seeking requires two points, that would cost 2 percent of the $75,000, or $1,500 in cash at closing.

You may be asking why anybody would *want* to pay points. The answer: because paying more points up front would lower the loan's interest rate, saving thousands of dollars in interest over the life of the loan.

Here's how. Points actually bridge the financial gap between interest rates. For example, why would a lender make a loan at 7.5 percent for the same fees that she'd make a loan at 8 percent? It probably wouldn't happen. That's where points come in. They allow the lender to make loans at various interest rates without losing money!

How can you determine if you should pay points to get a lower interest rate or forget it and go ahead with the higher rate? (You know what's coming, don't you?) It depends on what you're trying to achieve. If I know that I can pay $500 in extra points at closing to get my interest rate lowered so that I'll pay $20 less in my monthly payment, here's how I calculate it. I take my monthly savings of $20 and divide it into the $500 cost of the points. It gives me 25, meaning 25 months. So my breakeven point is 25 months. If I think I'll keep the house and the loan for more than two years, I'll win by paying more points now. But if I sell the house or refinance the loan before that time, I'll lose money on the extra points I paid. Simple math will tell you if you can win or lose.

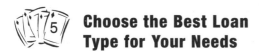 **Choose the Best Loan Type for Your Needs**

Shopping for the Best Conventional Fixed-Rate Loan

What it is. A conventional fixed-rate loan is financing where the interest rate remains the same for the life of the loan. Loan terms can run for 10, 15, 20, 30, or even (gulp) 40 years. Most conventional loans require that the borrower have a minimum down payment of 5 percent (unless he's using a 20 percent gift from a relative), good creditworthiness, and the ability to meet fairly stringent loan qualifying criteria.

Pros. The benefits of using a conventional fixed-rate mortgage include the following:

1. The interest rate remains stationary for the life of the loan.
2. Lenders may allow comortgagors or cosigners on conventional loans.
3. The lender may be willing to assist the borrower in funding a portion of the closing costs in return for a higher interest rate on the loan (this is called *premium pricing* and we'll cover it later in this Step).

4. If the loan requires private mortgage insurance, its premiums are generally less than those with ARM or FHA loans.
5. The lender may keep the loan "in portfolio" (not sell it to the secondary market) and thus be able to sidestep stiff underwriting guidelines.

Cons.   The negatives to using a conventional fixed-rate mortgage include the following:

1. The interest rate does not fluctuate during the life of the loan (even if interest rates drop).
2. Private mortgage insurance is required on most loans with a down payment of less than 20 percent.
3. Underwriting guidelines are tougher than with FHA or VA loans.
4. Qualifying ratios (28 percent and 36 percent) are tougher for buyers to meet than those for FHA or VA loans.
5. Interest rates, origination fees, and other loan costs are determined by lenders on an individual basis and could therefore be higher than similar programs in the marketplace.

Buyer profiles.   You may be a likely candidate for a conventional fixed-rate loan if you fit the following profile:

1. Have good to excellent credit and fairly low debts in proportion to your income.
2. Have a solid employment record (two-year minimum, which could include time in formal education for current position)
3. Have a down payment of at least 5 percent (or a gift of 20 percent or more from a relative)
4. Have money available for closing costs
5. Can qualify for a loan where no more than 28 percent of your gross monthly income goes to your house payment and no more than 36 percent of your monthly gross income goes toward your long-term debt (your house payment plus debts that can't be paid off in less than ten months)
6. Don't need a lot of special underwriting considerations
7. Desire a fixed-rate mortgage (for financial or emotional predictability)

8. Might establish a business relationship (or expand an existing one) with a lender willing to keep the loan in portfolio (This will sidestep paying taxes and insurance monthly in the loan payment and/or asking the lender to waive the private mortgage insurance on the loan.)

Little-known facts about conventional fixed-rate loans:

1. If a relative gives you 20 percent of the purchase price as a gift for the down payment on your loan, you don't have to use any of your own cash for the down payment.
2. Lenders can use a variety of "compensating factors" to write an otherwise imperfect loan (we'll cover these later in this Step).
3. A borrower living with a relative can use a 5 percent gift from that relative for the down payment on a house for the borrower. (Only the borrower would be on the loan, not the relative, nor would the relative have to qualify; for example, a son living with his mother.)
4. If you are purchasing an energy-efficient home (as determined by appraisal standards), you can increase your qualifying ratios by 2 percent on both the monthly payment and the long-term debt ratio (28 percent becomes 30 percent and 36 percent becomes 38 percent).

Questions to ask the lender.   When considering a conventional fixed-rate loan, ask the lender the following questions:

1. What concessions are you willing to make to get my business? (You may be pleasantly surprised!)
2. Since the secondary market doesn't require that I have tax and insurance accounts on my loan, can't we waive these, allowing me to pay them outside the loan?
3. Would you be willing to keep my loan in portfolio, allowing me to sidestep private mortgage insurance on the loan? (The lender might agree to this but charge a little higher interest rate on the loan.)

You'll find a Conventional Loan Qualifying Form at Figure 8.3.

FIGURE 8.3   Conventional Loan Qualification Form

Sale Price   (1) _____

    Less Loan Amount   (2) _____   Equals Required Down Payment $ _____

Estimated Closing Costs *Plus* Estimated Prepaid Escrow   + _____

    Total Closing Cost $ _____

Less Cash on Deposit   – _____

Required Cash To Close $ _____

    (2) _____ Divided by (1) _____ Equals LTV _____ %

Gross Income (Mortgagor) _____ and (Comortgagor) _____ = $ _____ (A)

Proposed Housing Expense:

    Principal and Interest $ _____

    Other Financing   _____

    Hazard Insurance   _____

    Taxes   _____

    Mortgage Insurance   _____

    Homeowners Association Fees   _____

    Other: _____   _____

Total Housing Payment   _____   (B)

Total Obligations (Beyond Ten Months)   _____   (C)

Total Housing Payment (B), *Plus* Monthly Obligations (C) =   _____   (D)

    (B) _____ Divided by (A) _____ = _____ %   Housing Ratio

    (D) _____ Divided by (A) _____ = _____ %   Total Debt Ratio

---

Consider Private Mortgage Insurance

What it is.   Private mortgage insurance (PMI) insures the lender against the borrower's default on a conventional mortgage. It is generally required when the down payment on the loan is less than 20 percent and/or at the lender's request (as in the case of marginally qualified buyers, marginal property, or both).

Pros.   The benefits to using private mortgage insurance include the following:

1. It may help you purchase property with less than a 20 percent down payment.
2. The cost of PMI is typically less than that of mortgage insurance required under FHA.
3. PMI may be removed from the loan (based on the lender's requirements).
4. A portion of the paid premium may be rebated, depending on the type of PMI payment plan you choose.

Cons.   The negatives to using private mortgage insurance include the following:

1. Upfront costs are added to closing as well as monthly costs on the PITI payment.
2. PMI can only be removed if the lender's removal criteria are met (on a case-by-case basis).
3. PMI is not tax deductible.

Buyer profiles.   You may be a likely candidate to use PMI in your loan if you fit the following profile:

1. Have a minimal down payment (less than 20 percent, depending on the loan)
2. Want to use a conventional fixed-rate or an adjustable rate loan
3. Want to purchase a single-family residence
4. Don't need a lot of special underwriting considerations

Questions to ask the lender.   Before deciding to pay private mortgage insurance with your loan, ask the lender the following questions:

1. How many PMI companies do you shop with and do you try to get the borrower the lowest premium?
2. What are the current guidelines for removing PMI from a mortgage?
3. Are there currently any alternatives for PMI with your company (e.g., portfolio lending)?

Shopping for the Best Adjustable-Rate Mortgage

What it is.   An adjustable-rate mortgage (ARM) is a type of conventional, non-fixed-rate loan that adjusts based on fluctuations in the economy. It is tied to an index (an indicator of inflation); the interest rate is usually calculated by adding the index (such as Treasury securities or T-bills, etc.) to a margin (which is the lender's cost of doing business plus profit).

$$\text{Index} + \text{Margin} = \text{Loan's interest rate}$$

Pros.   The benefits to using an adjustable rate mortgage include the following:

1. The interest rate adjusts based on economic fluctuations.
2. Typically, such loans have lower initial rates than fixed-rate conventional loans.
3. Because the lender makes a higher profit, the borrower can often get underwriting concessions on ARM programs.

Cons.   The negatives to using an adjustable rate mortgage include the following:

1. The interest rate adjusts based on economic swings.
2. Borrowers who have infrequent pay increases could find themselves financially burdened to make payment increases.
3. Special loan options (such as the ability to convert them to fixed-rate loans) can prove expensive if not chosen to meet the borrower's needs.

Buyer profiles.   You may be a likely candidate for an ARM if you fit the following profile:

1. Will keep the house/loan only a short time
2. Don't need the security of a fixed-rate mortgage
3. Expect that income increases will keep pace with payment adjustments
4. Cannot qualify at market rates and/or want to purchase a home that is slightly out of your financial reach

5. Feel that inflation will remain under control (since payment increases are a by-product of increasing inflation)
6. Want the loan interest rate to fluctuate downward to mirror changes in the economy

Little-known facts about adjustable rate mortgages:

1. ARMs are the most likely loans for the lender to keep in portfolio (since their fluctuation can generate the greatest potential profit for the lender).
2. If an ARM program has an option to convert to a fixed-rate loan, it adjusts not to current market rates, but based on a formula that generally creates a higher-than-market interest rate.
3. Shopping for the margin is just as important as shopping for the index, since the margin remains constant for the life of the loan, no matter how the index fluctuates.
4. As a marketing tool, a lender can provide a starting or "teaser" rate that is deeply discounted for the first year of the loan.

Questions to ask the lender.   Before deciding on an ARM loan, ask the lender the following questions:

1. Which indices are available for your ARM programs?
2. What are the margins on various ARM programs you offer?
3. What are the various adjustment periods on ARMs you offer (i.e., one year, three years, seven years, etc.)?
4. How can I determine if my payment adjustment is correct? (Most lenders have toll-free telephone numbers you can call to have the payment recalculated.)

You'll find an ARM Qualifying Form in Figure 8.4.

Shopping for the Best Federal Housing Administration Loan

What it is.   Federal Housing Administration (FHA) financing is a type of federally insured loan that indemnifies the lender against the borrower's default. It was created by the U.S. Department of Housing and Urban Development (HUD) as a way to boost home ownership among moderate-income Americans.

FIGURE 8.4   Adjustable-Rate Mortgage Qualification Form

Sale Price   (1) _____
   Less Loan Amount   (2) _____   Equals Required Down Payment $ _____

Estimated Closing Costs *Plus* Estimated Prepaid Escrow   + _____

   Total Closing Cost $ _____

Less Cash on Deposit   − _____

Required Cash To Close $ _____

   (2) _____   Divided by (1) _____   Equals LTV _____ %

Gross Income (Mortgagor) _____ and (Comortgagor) _____ = $ _____ (A)

Proposed Housing Expense:

   Principal and Interest $ _____

   Other Financing   _____

   Hazard Insurance   _____

   Taxes   _____

   Mortgage Insurance   _____

   Homeowners Association Fees   _____

   Other: _____   _____

Total Housing Payment   _____   (B)

Total Obligations (Beyond Ten Months)   _____   (C)

Total Housing Payment (B), *Plus* Monthly Obligations (C) =   _____   (D)

   (B) _____   Divided by (A) _____ = _____ %   Housing Ratio

   (D) _____   Divided by (A) _____ = _____ %   Total Debt Ratio

---

Pros.   The benefits of using an FHA loan include the following:

1. Qualifying guidelines can be more flexible because they serve the general homebuyer. (Current qualifying ratios are 29 percent and 41 percent).
2. FHA loans offer flexibility for borrowers who have had previous credit blemishes and/or bankruptcy.

3. A low down payment is the hallmark of the FHA loan. You only need 3 percent down on acquisition prices of $50,000 or less. For prices exceeding $50,000, the down payment is 3 percent of the first $25,000 and 5 percent of the balance (up to your geographical area's maximum).

Cons.   The negatives of using an FHA loan include the following:

1. The FHA mortgage insurance premium (MIP) covers the entire loan for its life. It includes a fee equal to 2.5 percent of the loan amount (which can be paid in cash at closing or financed into the loan) plus an annual premium of .5 percent, paid monthly in the payment.
2. Because of fairly stringent property guidelines, some properties are not available for FHA financing or need work repairs in order to qualify.
3. Maximums on purchase prices (by geographical region) make FHA not a viable resource in some parts of the country.

Buyer profile.   You may be a likely candidate for an FHA loan if you fit the following profile:

1. Have a minimal down payment
2. Are moderately qualified but need a lower-than-market interest rate to aid in qualifying
3. Need underwriting assistance to compensate for credit gliches, previous bankruptcy, and/or previous fore-closure
4. Desire to or now working with a seller or other third party to pay part or all of the closing costs and prepaids
5. Want an insured loan (in which some of the mortgage insurance premium might eventually be rebated to you)
6. Want a loan that could be assumed (with qualifying) should you desire to sell

Little-known facts about FHA loans:

1. While there is no prepayment penalty on FHA loans, you do need to give FHA a 30-day notice before paying off a loan, or an interest penalty (equal to a month's worth of interest) will apply.

2. A borrower can have more than one FHA loan at a time.
3. FHA has a streamlined refinance program for lowering the interest rate on an existing FHA loan
4. FHA has a work-out program to assist borrowers who become delinquent in their mortgage payments.

Questions to ask the lender.   Before deciding on an FHA loan, ask the lender the following questions:

1. What interest rate and corresponding points are currently available on your FHA loans?
2. Which closing costs do I *have* to pay? (Many are negotiable with the seller or other third party.)
3. Do you specialize in FHA loans and, if so, what is your average closing time for them?

You'll find an FHA Qualifying Form in Figure 8.5.

Shopping for the Best Department of Veterans Affairs or VA Loan

What it is.   A VA loan is a type of mortgage loan made to veterans. It provides a guarantee to the lender against the borrower's default.

Pros.   The benefits in using a VA loan include the following:

1. No down payment is required (based on the applicant's qualifications).
2. No private mortgage insurance is required.
3. Discount points can be negotiated between buyer and seller.
4. Closing costs favor the veteran-borrower because some costs must be paid by the seller or other third party.
5. VA loans can be used by National Guard/reservists who qualify.
6. You can have more than one VA loan at a time (but must reside on the property when first purchased).

FIGURE 8.5 Federal Housing Administration Qualifying Guidelines

---

		Borrower	Coborrower	Total
Monthly Income		$ _____	$ _____	$ _____

Housing Ratio		**Fixed Payment Ratio**	
Principal and Interest	$ _____	Total Housing Expenses	$ _____
Real Estate Taxes	+ _____	Monthly Installment	+ _____
Hazard Insurance	+ _____	Revolving Accounts	+ _____
FHA MIP (If Financed)	+ _____		+ _____
Other (Homeowners Association Fees, Condo Fees, LIDs)	+ _____	Other Recurring Charges	+ _____
		Total Fixed Payments	$ _____
Total Housing Expense	$ _____	Ratio (Divide Fixed Payment by Income)	$ _____
Ratio (Divide Housing Expense by Income)	_____ %		

Acceptable Ratio: 29%　　　　　　　　　**Acceptable Ratio: 41%**

Note: Ratios can be exceeded when compensating factors such as the following are present:

　　—Large down payment
　　—Substantial cash reserves
　　—Low overall debt
　　—Excellent job history
　　—History of managing high housing expenses
　　—Purchasing an energy-efficient house

Cons.　The negatives in using a VA loan include the following:

1. Even though the lender is guaranteed against the veteran's default on the loan, the veteran must indemnify the federal government (pay them back) for any loss incurred due to the veteran's loan default.
2. The borrower must intend to reside on the property in order to use a VA loan.
3. A loan funding fee applies to VA loans and costs more if you have used a VA loan previously and/or are a National Guard member or reservist.

4. The veteran-borrower is only released from liability on the loan when it's paid off or another veteran substitutes his/her entitlement for that of the borrower-veteran.

Buyer profile.   You may be a likely candidate for a VA loan if you fit the following profile:

1. Are a veteran who is a first-time or subsequent purchaser
2. Have little or no down payment
3. Want a loan that is guaranteed by the federal government
4. Are looking for the seller or other third party to assist in paying all or part of the closing costs
5. Are looking for a loan with no mortgage insurance premium
6. Want a loan that is assumable (with qualifying) should you sell

Little-known facts about VA loans:

1. If a borrower refinances out of a VA loan (but still keeps the property), the veteran's eligibility initially used to obtain that loan will not be released until the veteran "deeds out" (sells) that property.
2. As with other loans, the borrower can pay discount points to obtain a lower rate of interest.
3. An unremarried widow or widower of a veteran who died in active duty or due to a service-related injury may be able to finance one single-family residence property using a VA loan.
4. The funding fee on VA loans is waived for veterans with any amount of disability as well as for widow/widowers of veterans using the program.
5. A veteran who has purchased previously and has one or more VA loans outstanding may still have leftover eligibility to be able to purchase again. (Your lender can calculate this for you.)

Questions to ask the lender.   Before deciding on a VA loan, ask the lender the following questions:

1. What percentage of your company's business is made up of VA loans? (A lender who makes only a small number

of VA loans may not be as adept at getting them closed and could end up causing delays for the borrower. The key: place your loan with a high volume VA lender.)

2. Is your company a direct endorsement lender? (The VA allows certain qualified lenders to make approval decisions on their own. This can speed up the loan approval process significantly.)

3. Which loan and closing fees am I *not* allowed to pay for in a VA loan? (Since a progressive VA lender would know the answer to this question, it's a great way to test the experience level of this company where VA loans are concerned.)

A VA Qualifying Form is provided in Figure 8.6.

Considering a Community Homebuyer Program Loan

What it is.   The Community Home Buyer (CHB) loan programs were born out of the national Community Redevelopment Act several years ago. Their focus is to provide affordable housing to moderate-income Americans. The original program was originated by Fannie Mae in the secondary market and is called the 3/2 Option Plan. This meant that 3 percent of the down payment needed to come from the borrower's funds, but the remaining 2 percent (of the total 5 percent) could come from a relative's gift, an employer, or a community housing bond fund. CHB loans are typically written using conventional or FHA loan criteria. Today CHB programs flourish, because lenders are able to design their own in-house programs that can be sold to and recycled by the secondary market.

Pros.   The benefits of using a CHB loan program include the following:

1. The programs allow lower qualifying guidelines with ratios of approximately 33 percent+ for house payment and 38 percent+ for total long-term debt (exceeding those of conventional fixed-rate loans).

FIGURE 8.6   VA Buyer Income Qualification Form

Loan Amount $ _____

Gross Income per Month (Veteran or Spouse) $ _____ (A)
(including pension compensation or other *net* income)

Less: Federal Income Tax $ _____
         State Income Tax   _____

         Social Security Tax   _____
         Other   _____

Net Take-Home Pay $ _____ (B)

Housing Expense:

         House Payment $ _____
         (Principal and Interest)
         Taxes   + _____

         Insurance   + _____
         HOA/Assessments   + _____

             Subtotal $ _____ (C)

         Utilities $ _____

         Other (pool, air-conditioning, etc.) + _____
         Maintenance   + _____

             Total Housing Expense $ _____ (D)

Fixed Obligations:
         Total of all monthly debt payments
         which will last six months or longer
         including "job-related expenses" $ _____ (E)

Balance Remaining for Family Support (B less D and E) $ _____

                                     Family Support
         Number of Family Members _____ Balance Required $ _____
                                     (refer to Figure 8.1)

Ratio: (C plus E)   Divided by (A) $ _____ = Ratio _____ %*
                                                       (round down to two digits)

*A statement that lists all compensating factors that justify approval must be provided if ratio exceeds 41 percent unless the residual income exceeds the required amount by at least 20 percent.

2. Depending on the loan program, the borrower may need a down payment of only 3 percent with the balance waived or coming from housing bond funds, or a forgivable loan from the lender, if certain loan criteria are met.
3. Programs can make underwriting exceptions, especially for nontraditional employment (e.g., seasonal workers).

Cons. The negatives of using a CHB loan program include the following:

1. In order to provide loans to a certain quadrant of homebuyers, maximums are set geographically for income as well as home price.
2. Because house price maximums are set by area, this program is not widely used where housing costs have escalated.
3. Before closing the CHB loan, the applicant may be required to attend home purchasing classes or complete a workbook course to help educate the buyer on what it takes financially to be a homeowner. This can be a positive!

Buyer profile. You may be a likely candidate for a CHB loan if you fit the following profile:

1. Have a small down payment (3 percent)
2. Are qualified to purchase a median-priced property in your area
3. Have explainable gaps in your employment picture
4. Are employed at a nontraditional job (e.g., seasonal worker or permanent part-time worker)
5. Need some concessions for qualifying, because of less-than-perfect credit, high debt ratios, etc.

Little-known facts about CHB loans:

1. Many lenders write CHB loans, but may call them by various names. Lenders may reference them by their own company name, such as the Home America program or First Time Buyer program.
2. Lenders are encouraged to participate in community housing development programs since they enrich the community—therefore, underwriting exceptions can often be made.

Questions to ask the lender.   Before deciding on a CHB loan, ask the lender the following questions:

1. Will you require me to complete the homebuyer class before closing the loan? Is it mandatory that I take the class in a formal classroom setting, or could I complete a manual instead at my own pace?
2. How do CHB loans differ from conventional or FHA loans? How do the closing costs compare to those of FHA?

You can use the conventional loan qualifying form (Figure 8.3) to qualify for the Community Home Buyers loan program. Just make sure you adjust the ratios to reflect 33 percent (instead of 28 percent) and 38 percent (instead of 36 percent).

Other Loans You Might Consider

Balloon loan.   A balloon loan has a date when the entire remaining balance on the loan is due—or the loan is up (just like a balloon). A lender may offer a three-, five-, or seven-year balloon at a fairly attractive interest rate, knowing that you'll be a short-term owner or one who can make other financing provisions during that time. On some balloon loans, there is a conversion option to either an adjustable- or fixed-rate loan when the balloon is due. Know the exact terms of the balloon loan and have a pretty good idea what your circumstances will be when the balloon comes due. Ask the lender if you'll have to qualify again to meet any conversion privileges, what the cost will be (if anything), and what could happen if you aren't able to meet the balloon loan requirements.

Two-step mortgage.   This Fannie Mae program is particularly attractive to first-time buyers, military families, and those who are frequently relocated. It works (as its name applies) in two steps. The first step offers a lower interest rate for the first five or seven years, based on the program you choose. At the end of the term of the first step, the interest rate is reset for the remainder of the loan. The new rate becomes an adjustable-rate mortgage, based on a formula tied to U.S. ten-year Treasury securities. The benefits of this program are that the interest rate is lower in the loan's early years, no additional fees are charged when the loan converts, and the borrower need not requalify when the loan resets. The two-step loan is a good program for short-term owners or marginal buyers who need a little more qualifying help.

Graduated payment loan.   This loan does exactly what its name denotes: the payments increase over time to a maximum, or plateau, and then remain there for the balance of the loan. While the loan is amortized over the loan term, the borrower can leverage up front by paying only a portion of the payment (which typically covers only a portion of the interest in the early stages of the loan). This means that should you need to sell early on, your loan may not have reduced much, if any! Ask the lender if this loan has negative amortization (where the shortfall of the payment is added monthly to the loan balance). Also make sure that you'll not need to sell too soon and/or you're making a significant down payment so that you won't have to bring a check to closing if you do have to sell during the early stages of the loan.

Biweekly mortgage.   Biweekly mortgages allow the borrower to make one-half of the regular payment every two weeks. This payment system adds a full additional payment each year (52 weeks in the year divided by a payment every 2 weeks equals 26 one-half payments, or 13 full payments!). This causes a 30-year loan to typically pay off in approximately 22 years. Most biweekly mortgages use payment withdrawal directly from your checking or savings account. Be sure to investigate (and object to) any additional fees for doing this, since the lender already has use of your money by this early-pay system! If you don't go with this particular type of loan, sure, you can make prepayments (note our information on this in Step #10). But the biweekly is a type of forced savings program to ensure that you do this on a regular, two-week schedule.

Low-doc/no-doc loan.   A low-doc/no-doc loan is one that requires less documentation (docs) than a standard loan. Depending on the type of loan (and the risk the lender is willing to take), these loans often require only a credit check and an appraisal, but not the standard employment, deposit, or income verifications.

So what's the catch: why would a lender in his/her right mind do this? The trade-off is that the borrower is usually required to make a down payment of 25 to 30 percent or more in order to off-set the lender's risk. Low-doc/no-doc loans do serve a segment of the homebuying crowd, such as the self-employed, who often have trouble documenting cash flow and providing suitable profit and loss paperwork to convince a lender under standard loan processing. While you may need to do some asking around to find the best lender with a good product (and a competitive interest rate), low-doc/no-doc loans are out there.

Loans tied to other collateral.   If you can't get a mortgage loan (and/or don't want the house tied up as collateral), there are other potential sources of funding.

You could use a business loan to fund your home purchase, tied to other assets like stocks or bonds. The downside here is that, depending on your lender, the rate may be 1.5 to 2 percent over prime, probably an adjustable-rate loan (for the most lender profit), and could be only short-term (three to five years) but possibly with a rollover renewal clause.

The biggest detriment is that since the house isn't used as collateral, you won't have the mortgage interest deductibility factor if you use a business loan. Also, the business loan will tie up other collateral that could prevent you from liquidating those assets and/or borrowing against them until the loan is paid in full.

A little later in this Step, we'll cover more ideas on creative financing opportunities, especially if the lender is saying "no" to your mortgage request.

The Best Test for Choosing the Best Mortgage for You

We'll end this section as we started—reminding you that before you can choose the most cost-effective loan, you've got to know what it is you want to accomplish. Once you have that in mind (i.e., short-term ownership, quick equity build-up, or a loan to fund "your final resting place"—on earth, that is!) you can choose the loan that best meets those needs.

Figures don't lie. That's why it's imperative to ask your lender to prepare cost comparisons for you. We've provided you a Loan Comparison Worksheet in Figure 8.7 to assist you. Happy loan hunting!

FIGURE 8.7 Loan Comparison Worksheet

	Loan Type		
	Conventional	**FHA**	**VA**
Sale Price . . . . $_____			
Interest Rate . . . . $_____			
Down Payment . . . . $_____			
Total Loan to be Amortized . . . . $_____			

Estimated Loan Costs

MIP (Unless FHA Included Above) . . . . $_____			
Loan Origination Fee . . . . $_____			
Assumption Fee . . . . $_____			
Credit Report . . . . $_____			
Appraisal Fee . . . . $_____			
Recording Fee . . . . $_____			
Title (ALTA) Policy (Use Loan Amount) . . . $_____			
Attorney Fee . . . . $_____			
Escrow Closing Fee . . . . $_____			
Interest Proration . . . . $_____			
Tax Proration . . . . $_____			
Fire and Hazard Insurance 1st year . . . . $_____			
Lender's Application Fee . . . . $_____			
Purchaser's Buydown Points . . . . $_____			
Long-Term Escrow Set-up Fee . . . . $_____			
Tax Service Fee . . . . $_____			
Misc., LID, City Code, Reserves . . . . $_____			
Home Inspection Fee . . . . $_____			
Total Estimated Closing Costs . . . . $_____			

Reserves and Prorates

Property Taxes (Minimum 2 Months) . . . . . . $_____			
Fire and Hazard Insurance (Min. 2 Mths.) $_____			
Mortgage Insurance . . . . $_____			
Total Reserves and Prorates . . . . $_____			
Total Cash Outlay . . . . $_____			

Estimated Monthly Payment

Principal and Interest . . . . $_____			
Tax Reserves . . . . $_____			
Insurance Reserves . . . . $_____			
MIP Insurance (Unless FHA Included Above) . . . . $_____			
Total Estimated Monthly Payment . . . . $_____			

The undersigned hereby acknowledges receipt of a copy of this estimation.

By _____ Signed _____ Date _____

You've checked out the loan programs, but still have questions. So IT'S YOUR MOVE ♣

 ## Determine When to Lock In the Interest Rate

One of the biggest (and earliest) questions you may be asked as a mortgage applicant for a new loan is, "Do you want to lock in the interest rate, or let it float?" In real estate "slanguage" this means that if you like where the interest rate is right now, you can commit to it. But if you don't and rates happen to increase, you'd be stuck with the higher interest rate (assuming you could qualify at that rate!).

So the options are the following:

1. You could lock in an interest rate and be assured that your interest rate wouldn't increase.
2. You could make no decision and hope that rates come down (or at least don't increase).
3. And if rates did increase, you'd have to hope that you could still qualify for the loan!

Given these questions, answers, and roulette scenario, you can see why a majority of buyers do lock in their interest rates, especially under interest-volatile conditions.

Before you do lock in your rate, however, be sure you ask the lender the following questions:

1. How long will it take to close my loan and will this lock-in give us enough time? (Obviously, you don't want to be locking in for only 45 days if the loan closing isn't projected to occur for 60 days).
2. If I don't lock in now and the interest rate does increase, can I still qualify? At what interest rate would I *not* be able to qualify? (This gives you parameters. For example, if rates have been fairly stable and it would take an interest increase of more than 2 percent before you could no longer qualify, you may still be able to qualify—but you *would* be paying more interest!)

3. Is there a fee for locking in? When is it paid? (Many lenders have either dropped their fees for locking in or will "negotiate" them with you.)
4. Do you have a lock-in that would float down if interest rates drop? (In today's competitive market, many lenders are willing to float the rate downward if rates drop. This keeps the borrower happy and less likely to jump ship midstream to another loan program or lender.)
5. What have been the interest rate trends on this type of loan and what is projected? (You can also arm yourself with information by checking sources like the money rate section of the *Wall Street Journal.* Pay particular attention to actions of the Federal Reserve Board (which loosens or tightens money in circulation) and short-term sources that have an effect on interest rates, such as fluctuations of the ten-year Treasury note.
6. Don't forget the discussion we had earlier about paying more points versus capturing a lower rate of interest. In general, if you think you'll own the property and loan a short period of time, paying lower points is usually more cost effective. Conversely, long-term ownership favors paying more points to buy the interest rate down.

If you've made your decision about locking in the interest rate, then IT'S YOUR MOVE ✦

 ## Ask for Concessions from the Lender

It's a fact that lenders want to lend money—that's how they make money. But it doesn't mean that the consumer always has to stand pat for the terms, conditions, even the interest rate that the lender makes available.

That's where concessions come in. They're bargaining tools to help reach a middle ground between what the lender wants to make (profitwise) on the loan and what you're willing to pay for the loan package.

Possible Areas to Negotiate with the Lender

We've already addressed two of the most logical areas of negotiation with the lender: interest rates and points. The bottom line is that at the rate and points initially quoted by the lender, he or she will make a certain profit. But it doesn't necessarily mean that the lender wouldn't make a profit by accepting less interest or fewer points. It would just be lower than the maximum profit possible.

Here's a comparison. When lenders sell loans (which most of them do) to the secondary mortgage market, they do so at a discount for the privilege of getting the loan recycled to cash now. Depending on how strong the loans are, the secondary market might ask for a larger discount to compensate for the risk.

So if you barter with the lender to reduce the interest rate and/or the points you pay, you are in essence doing the same thing as the secondary market—making a statement to the lender that if he/she wants your business, it will be on a two-sided negotiated basis.

If you aren't brave enough to negotiate for the big impact items like interest and points, how about the smaller potatoes of warehousing fees, underwriting fees, and other items that fit into the category of "garbage fees." These charges vary greatly from lender to lender and are often pricey for the service that's rendered. So use the Good Faith Estimate of costs provided you by the lender to see what you can negotiate and eliminate.

Premium Pricing: A Possible Leverage Tool

Let's say that your loan qualifying looks pretty good, but you're $500 short on covering the closing costs, and you've tapped out the seller. Where else can you turn? You may be able to get the extra closing cost leverage you need from your lender by a system called *premium pricing.*

Here's how it works. The lender states willingness to pay or waive the last $500 of the closing costs for you. The only catch is that you'll be charged ⅛ percent more interest on the loan, thus premium pricing. You pay a premium for paying *fewer* closing costs! The advantage is that you get the loan and you don't have to scrape up the missing $500. The disadvantage is that the $500 you were short may end up costing you thousands of dollars more on the loan.

There is a time and a place for premium pricing, especially if it means the difference between getting the loan and not getting the loan. Be sure to calculate exactly what the "premium" is costing you and whether it can be offset by other rewards.

Portfolio Lending

Portfolio lending is discussed early in this Step, but it's worth discussing in depth with the following example.

Jane and Tom Byers have been depositors with ABC Bank for many years. They are now searching for their first home loan and think immediately of the bank. Being savvy consumers (who have read this book), they ask the lender if there's any way he can make exceptions such as waiving the private mortgage insurance and letting them pay their taxes and insurance payments outside the loan. They are pleasantly surprised when the lender says "yes," based in part on their long-standing relationship with the bank. The lender will write the loan as a portfolio loan, keeping it in house and not selling it into the secondary mortgage market. This means that certain exceptions to traditional underwriting (like waiving the private mortgage insurance) can be made.

A fairy tale? Maybe not. Lenders today know that replacing existing customers is much more expensive than keeping the ones they have. That's why if a lender has the capacity to keep loans in portfolio, it's often customers with sound track records of doing business with the bank who benefit.

But what about the buyer who can't meet the standard loan qualifying guidelines? Could he ever obtain a portfolio loan? Possibly. The lender knows that there are certain borrowers and situations that may not meet the underwriting guidelines required by the secondary market, but nevertheless do make reasonable sense as a mortgage risk. These could include a borrower with too little time on the job, a self-employed borrower who has high debt ratios, or a rural property to be financed that has more than the normal-sized lot.

What types of loans are the most likely to be portfolio loans? Often adjustable-rate mortgages, since they typically have the highest amount of profit to the lender. The least likely loans are probably government-insured (FHA) and guaranteed (VA) loans.

As with all concessions, the key is "If you don't ask, you don't get." And if you ask and don't get the first time, it doesn't mean that it's not doable—you just may have the wrong loan type, the wrong lender, or an ill-fitting combination of the two.

Once you've negotiated concessions with the lender, you still may need some qualifying room. If so, IT'S YOUR MOVE ♣

 ## Use "Compensating Factors" to Get the Loan You Want

You get the phone call that everyone dreads—the lender calls to say that he can't qualify you for the loan you wanted. What can you do now?

Besides asking "Why not?" don't panic. Ask the lender if he considered your *compensating factors*. These are extra factors like "bonus points" that make an otherwise marginal borrower strong and often can make the difference between getting a loan and not getting one.

Even though compensating factors will vary by loan program and lender, below are the most common ones used by the majority of lenders who sell their loans to the secondary mortgage market.

The applicant

1. is making a large down payment;
2. demonstrates the ability to devote a greater portion of income to housing expenses (for example, you're trying to qualify for a $1,200 payment and have been paying rent on time in that amount for the past two years);
3. is purchasing a property that qualifies as "energy efficient" (which is determined by appraisal standards);
4. is able to show a consistent pattern of saving;
5. has maintained a good credit history;
6. has a low-debt or no-debt position;
7. can demonstrate a potential for increased earnings because of education and/or job training;
8. has substantial net worth;
9. is purchasing a home due to corporate relocation of a primary wage earner and the secondary wage earner (with a previous work history) is expected to return to work; and/or

10. has short-term income (child support, Social Security) that traditionally is not counted in qualifying because it would not continue three years beyond the date of the mortgage application.

Just look at all the resources you can call upon to make the loan work! If you still need more qualifying room, IT'S YOUR MOVE ⤵

 ## Increase Your Down Payment and/or Decrease Your Debt to Get Loan Approval

The lender has tried all the compensating factors and is still not convinced that you can qualify. He suggests that you try to increase your down payment and/or decrease your debt to meet the qualifying guidelines. Here are some ideas for doing just that!

1. See if the seller (or other third party) would be willing to contribute to the closing costs.
2. Get a gift to help out with the down payment and/or closing costs. Although this typically has to come from a relative, your employer might be able to contribute (depending on the type of loan).
3. Refinance an asset such as personal property to free up cash. This might also help your debt ratio if you could reduce the interest rate and lower the monthly payment by increasing the payment period.
4. Put a lien on an asset (but be careful not to create more long-term debt for qualifying in the process). Borrow against a boat, car, or life insurance policy. With permission, you could also put a lien on a relative's asset (stock, bonds) to create cash. This is best accomplished when the borrower is co-owner of an asset, such as stocks, bonds, or certificates of deposit.
5. Barter a service, use sweat equity (labor contributions) for part of the down payment or closing costs. For example, a painter could contribute work in lieu of a seller having to pay someone to repaint.
6. Transfer the use of an item. Depending on the type of loan you're seeking, you might be able to get a builder ⸾

more points by allowing her to use your travel trailer for a summer in exchange.

7. Use a coborrower or cosigner to reduce the amount of the loan you need to qualify for.

8. Use a pledged account: Pledge other assets (such as a boat, travel trailer, or a relative's assets) to the lender for additional collateral.

9. Don't go on vacation—work instead! If you get the loan, you'll need to hang around to move anyway!

10. Call in your markers. If someone owes you money (even if it will come to you in monthly payments), ask for it now. If it can be documented, the lender may consider it as a compensating factor to push your qualifying over the edge!

Suggestions If the Lender Says Your Debt Is Too High

1. Pay off a debt. Use cash or another asset to alleviate the debt.

2. Sell the asset that has debt against it.

3. Pay down a debt. Most lenders consider a long-term debt to be anything that can't be paid off in ten months or is continuous in nature. If you pay it down below this point, that payment may be subtracted from your long-term debt picture.

4. Refinance a high-rate loan.

5. Consolidate your loans. (Note: Discuss this with the lender *before* doing it as some lenders see it as a negative, indicating that you can't manage the debt you have.) This strategy can be advantageous if you lower the monthly payment, lower the interest rate, and make the debt more manageable.

6. Close out credit accounts you aren't using. Ask the lender if this might shore up your qualifying picture since he might be counting a minimum monthly repayment against each one of the open accounts (even those that have zero balances).

If you've used all your "aces" with the lender, IT'S YOUR MOVE ✒

 **Alternatives to
Lender Financing**

If the lender says "no" and you've explored other lenders and other lender alternatives, it's still not time to give up financing your dream home. While lender financing is the most traditional approach to financing a home, it's not the sole approach. So let's investigate alternative sources to fund your purchase.

Seller financing.   Ask if the seller can carry all or part of the financing for you. Be prepared to make trade-offs like those we covered previously in Step #7—e.g., offering full price, giving the seller a high rate of interest, and excluding personal property that might make your request seem more equitable.

Reasons the seller might consider carrying all or part of the financing for you include the following:

- Tax considerations: On installment sales, the seller does not pay tax on the gain from the sale until he actually receives the payments.
- Increased sale price: Often the seller will not only receive top dollar for the property by carrying financing, but can also increase the yield on the total sale because of the interest he would receive over time.
- Good investment: Carrying financing can provide a good return on the seller's money, much higher than many other financial market investments.
- Lower closing costs: Closing costs are usually minimal with a seller-financed sale.

Part conventional loan/part seller financing (75/10/15).
If the seller says "no" to carrying all of the financing for you, here's an alternative—a 75 percent first mortgage, a 10 percent down payment, and the remaining 15 percent of the purchase price in seller financing (usually for approximately 5 to 15 years, depending on your negotiations). The lender may be more willing to qualify you for a 75 percent loan than for one at a higher loan-to-value ratio since he'd have less risk. Although you still have to qualify with the lender based on repayment of both the first and second loans, you would sidestep private mortgage insurance, which would save on your monthly payments.

Lease purchases.   If done properly, lease purchases can accommodate the needs of both buyer and seller. By definition, a lease purchase is a delayed closing under which the buyer takes occupancy under a lease prior to closing. In other words, it's a formal sale, just with a future closing date (sometimes six months or more in the future). It's important to note that this is different from a lease option, which doesn't have to be exercised. To breach a lease purchase carries all of the ramifications of backing out of any other real estate purchase, including loss of earnest money, suit for specific performance, and other potential remedies by the seller.

You would be wise to have a real estate attorney draft or at least review the agreement since it should contain several provisions in order to work well. He or she will address the following:

- Remember, improvements prior to closing can be dangerous for the buyer because if the sale falls through, you would have improvements in the seller's property for which you might not be compensated.
- Who has insurance coverage? Usually the seller keeps insurance in place and the buyer adds an extra liability policy somewhat like renter's insurance.
- What are the provisions for default? Usually, whatever is stated in the standard purchase agreement prevails.
- Will there be a part of the monthly lease payment credited to the buyer? If so, will it reduce the purchase price or go towards the buyer's closing costs?

A sale using a lease purchase allows the seller to leave the property in a timely fashion (especially if needing to relocate for a job) while allowing the buyer time to meet the terms and conditions of the sale.

Make sure what you're trying to accomplish makes sense. Is buying time really going to make the difference? As the buyer, ask yourself the following questions:

1. Is the time frame for closing reasonable, given what I need to accomplish?
2. Have I been preliminarily qualified for the loan I need? Does it look as though the type of financing I need will be available to me?

3. If what I'm expecting to happen doesn't, do I have a backup plan so that I can complete the home purchase?

If you've met the ten challenges of "Choose the Best Loan," congratulations! IT'S YOUR MOVE to Step #9

But if you've fallen short of getting the loan together, GO TO THE PENALTY BOX:

Penalty Box

Possible penalties include the following:

1. Being saddled with a loan that's not cost effective and eventually causes you to default and lose the house
2. Paying too much in closing costs when you should have shopped around with various lenders for various types of loans
3. Roadblocked by financing because you stop with the first lender that says "no" and you don't investigate other creative solutions.

For "help" out of the PENALTY BOX:

1. Shop for loan closing costs, points, and loan terms just as diligently as you shop for the interest rate.
2. Ask the lender for written comparisons between loan types you're considering.
3. Turn a lender's "No" into a "Go" by exploring compensating factors, portfolio loans, and premium pricing.

 Take Trump Card #8

The biggest edge you'll have on home affordability for the long run is to shop tenaciously for a mortgage. Make sure that it fits your qualifying needs today as well as your economic needs for the future.

Step 9

Pick Up
the Keys

Your mortgage loan has been approved, the closing date has been set, you're almost ready to pick up the keys. But wait—you first need to do a property walk-through, secure your home-owner's insurance policy, and be prepared to ask questions at the closing so that you get answers to the remaining questions you have. We're rounding the last bend of the homebuying process—we can do it—so let's go!

 ## Do a Final Walk-Through
of the Property

It may have been a while since you've been to your new "home to be" or you could have dropped by yesterday. No matter, you need to do a final walk-through to make sure that everything is as you remembered it and that everything is in working order.

Most people are so anxious to close on their home that they often gloss over the final walk-through. I know this because I am a walk-through fatality!

On our last home purchase, we visited the property briefly before closing, mostly to see how our new furniture would look in the master bedroom, not to check out the mechanical aspects of the house where our focus should have been! In retrospect, I should have noticed that a 100-foot hose was draped around the side of the house, not out of the closest water faucet just feet away. After moving in, we discovered that not only was the rear water spigot not working, the pipe had burst on the interior wall, filling the office room in the basement with two inches of water. A dampening welcome to the new house and an expensive lesson to learn!

My new approach—no stone is too small to overturn in the final walk-through! I suggest that unless you want to learn a similar lesson, you do the same as well.

The walk-through usually occurs a day or so before the loan closing. But since that gives you precious little time to right a wrong if you find one, I suggest having the walk-through two or more days before closing. No matter when it's scheduled, make sure it's *before* the closing, not after. After that time you will have lost your leverage to object to things and, financially, will have played all your aces.

If you're working with a real estate agent, he/she will generally demand that the walk-through occur. But if you are working on your own and have not mentioned the walk-through to the seller (and/or have not placed it as a condition to your purchase agreement), you may meet some resistance. The request might intimate to the seller that you don't trust him or that he will skip out in the night with the personal property he promised to leave. No matter what the perception is, sell the walk-through to the seller. You can say, "It's one way to document that everything is as previously agreed in the contract. This will help relieve you of some liability, too, since we'll verify the working condition of the property before it's handed to me." If nothing else will convince the seller, this should.

It's also good to ask the seller to be gone from the property for the walk-through. Just as when you were viewing the home for the first time, this allows you the same freedom of discovery without someone looking over your shoulder.

What to Check For During the Walk-Through

What approach do you take and what should you look for when you do the walk-through? First of all, take the following paperwork with you:

1. The copy of the earnest money agreement
2. A copy of any listing agreement available
3. A copy of any seller property disclosure form
4. A copy of the home inspector's report (if applicable)

You'll want to take the following working items with you as well:

1. A flashlight
2. A tarp or other large cloth
3. A step stool
4. A tape measure
5. A night light
6. An extension cord

We'll explain how each of these is used.

Use a Systematic Approach to Checking the Property

If you use a systematic approach to checking the property, you won't forget vital items and you'll be able to log your findings in an orderly fashion.

If you viewed the home initially with another person, try to do the walk-through as a team as well. What you forget from before, the other person remembers.

View the home during the daytime as though you're seeing it for the first time. (If you can, it's good to go back at night to make sure that the external lighting is working as well.)

Inside the rooms.   As you move methodically through the rooms, note the following:

1. Is the house as physically sound as it looked before? Look for ceiling cracks, sloping floors, windows that are cracked or don't shut, and large amounts of bubbled or

peeling paint (which in the ceiling area could denote a leaky roof).

2. Use the flashlight to inspect unlighted closets.

3. Use the step stool to glance into attic areas (even if the home inspector did this before, things could have changed dramatically since that inspection).

4. Lie on the tarp to inspect any crawl (or crawly!) areas.

5. Use the night light to test each electric socket. Hold your hand over the sensor to test those on or near electric light fixtures as well as outlets on decks and patios.

6. Use the extension cord to plug in any floor lamps or other electrical personal property (generator, etc.) that will be left with the property.

7. If you're concerned about the size of the doorways for moving your personal effects and/or the size of the windows for curtains, now is a great time to use the tape measure to measure and record your findings.

8. Don't forget to look under area rugs, swing pictures out of the way, and look under beds as well—anything that could hide defects should be checked.

9. Use the paperwork you brought to review the condition of the property at the time of purchase, the personal property that will be left with the home, and the working condition of fixtures as described on the listing agreement or on the seller's property disclosure statement.

The mechanical aspects.   If you are going to give first priority to any of the inspection areas, this should be the one! These are not only the most crucial areas of concern, but also can be the most expensive to repair:

1. Furnace/heating unit: Turn on the furnace in the middle of summer and let it run for a while. If the heat is baseboard electric, make sure each unit works.

2. Air conditioner: Even if the snow is flying outside, turn on the air conditioner and/or any wall-unit air conditioners. (If it's winter, please be sure to remove any cover or insulation first!)

3. Ceiling fans: Try them on all speeds.

4. Water heater: Look around the unit for any current or old leaks. Check to see if there's a safety valve on the unit and if it appears in working order.
5. Plumbing fixtures: Flush all toilets, turn on all showers, and check the water pressure in all faucets.
6. Drains (especially in the basement and/or around the laundry area): Note any standing water that's near the drain, especially in a basement utility area that gets heavy use.
7. Garbage disposal: Turn it on.
8. Built-in appliances: Check all for working order (this is also a good time to ask the seller for any pamphlets or warranties that should be left with the appliances).
9. Other personal property left with house: If the lawnmower is being left, is it working? What about the garage-door opener? (By the way, don't forget to ask the seller to leave the remote for the garage door in the house.)

The exterior of the property.   Even if it's the dead of winter, you need to take a stroll around the house to check out the following:

1. Standing water around the foundation: Perhaps the ground is hard and water is running off; but it could also signal leaky pipes or other problems in or around the foundation/basement;
2. Water spigots: Unless they are weatherized, turn each on. Low water pressure could denote a leaky pipe as I learned by experience!
3. Condition of roof: Take a bird's-eye view from the ground or, if conditions permit, use a ladder to look on the roof. (Note: If it's winter and there's snow on the roof, check to see where the snow has melted the most. This is an indication that insulation may be poor in those areas.)
4. Condition of downspouts: Check to see if gutters are where they should be and if downspouts are attached to them.
5. Odors: A foul exterior order might mean that a septic system and/or drainfield is malfunctioning. (Note: If you do have a drainfield, it's good to ask the seller to point out its location and when they last had the septic tank pumped.)

6. Outbuildings: Are they as you remember them? If portable storage sheds are to be left, make sure they've been specified on the purchase agreement. (Other items that might be interpreted as personal property and thus "vanish" with the seller could include wood stoves, lawn jockeys (concrete statues), and dog kennels/runs.)

What If You Find Discrepancies?

That's what this walk-through is all about—making sure that the property is as you remembered it when you finalized the purchase agreement way back when!

The first step is to verify (using the paperwork) that there's been a change in the condition or circumstances.

Second, ask the seller (and real estate agent, if applicable) for his interpretation of this alteration.

Third, if you can't have a meeting of the minds about the item, get a third-party interpretation (the real estate agent, your attorney, the home inspector).

Fourth, if a meeting of the minds can't be reached and it's a big item worth fighting for and you want it rectified, refuse to close until the problem is taken care of to your satisfaction. If you aren't getting satisfaction now, what makes you think you'll have any more luck getting it *after* the closing gavel raps? But just as with your initial negotiations with the seller, know which battles are worth winning and which are more frivolous or ego based. You don't want to hold up the closing or risk losing the property over an issue that is truly more emotional than it is practical.

If the walk-through is complete and you're happy, then IT'S YOUR MOVE ♣

Prepare for the Closing

The good news is that these are the last items you'll have to work through and pull together before the house becomes yours. So here's a checklist of what you'll need and when to get it.

As soon as the loan is approved:

1. Give notice (if applicable) that you're moving (i.e., from your rental). If you're keeping a house to use as a rental, you may want to start the rental process on it now. And don't forget to check out a moving company. Depending on where you live, a month may not be enough notice to secure a date.

2. Get your homeowners insurance (and any other type of property insurance). By giving the insurance agent a copy of the listing agreement, she can write the policy, you can pay the first annual premium for it, and then you are ready to present the paid binder to the person closing your sale/mortgage loan. If a lender is giving you a mortgage, you'll need to make that lender the "loss payee" on the policy as well.

Prior to closing:

1. The closing agent will ask you to bring in a cashier's check for the balance of your down payment and your closing costs. Don't think that the closing agent doesn't trust you—it's just that a cashier's check will have no bank holds placed on it and can serve as cash in order to expedite payoff items for the seller and recording of new paperwork (title and deed) in your name.

2. As soon as the closing agent has them prepared, you can review the documents associated with the sale, including the preliminary title report, the financing documents, and the closing statements. (We'll explain these in detail in the next section.)

Looks like we're ready for your closing. So IT'S YOUR MOVE ♠

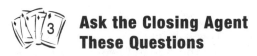 **Ask the Closing Agent These Questions**

Depending on the practices in your state and your local area, you may be closing the sale with the lender, a title company representative, a closing agent, or an attorney. Nevertheless, we'll cover some of the standard documents you'll review and sign and anticipate some of the questions you'll have as well.

What's on the HUD Settlement Statement?

Based on federal law, you have the right to inspect the HUD settlement form one business day prior to closing. While one day is the time required by law, most lenders won't object to providing the form to you earlier than that. This is suggested since it will give you time to sort out the potentially confusing form and structure your questions without the time pressures that occur at the closing table.

What will the settlement statement show? A lot. The idea behind the form is to show you exactly what your costs are, including the cost of arranging financing. This is also your final chance to get clarification for costs you see and/or want to object to (yes, that does happen sometime.)

Items on the HUD-1 Settlement Form

Costs you pay to get the loan and close the purchase:

1. Credit report fee: You undoubtedly paid this at the time of loan application.
2. Appraisal fee: You more than likely paid this as an upfront cost at loan application as well. Note: Since you paid for the appraisal, there's no harm in asking for a copy of it. The lender may balk, saying that it's needed for the loan package. You'll let the lender keep the original—all you're asking for is a copy of the appraisal you paid for!
3. Loan origination fee: This is the cost you pay for the privilege of getting the loan (and keeping the lender in business!). It covers the lender's costs of doing business and "originating" the loan. You'll usually see it expressed as a percent, such as 1 percent of the loan amount. In addition, you might see a lender charge an additional "underwriting" fee to compensate for his company's underwriting efforts.

4. Discount points: We covered these in depth in Step #8. One point is equal to 1 percent of the loan amount. Because points are a negotiable commodity from lender to lender, remember to shop diligently for the best buy.
5. Escrow closing fee: The title company or closing company charges this fee to prepare documents, collect and disburse funds, and orchestrate the closing activities.
6. Assumption fees: If you're assuming an existing loan on the property, there will more than likely be a fee for doing so.
7. Fees for recordation: These fees cover the recording of documents at the county recorder's office.
8. Tax service fee: A professional tax search company may be paid to review the property tax records and make sure the reserve account will be ample.
9. ALTA or lender's title insurance policy: If you're getting a new loan, the lender will require you to provide a policy of title insurance protecting the lender's interests.
10. Extended coverage title insurance: This type of title insurance protects the property against liens and other encumbrances that can show up after closing. It's important to consider purchasing this coverage, especially if you're purchasing a property that's had remodeling or additions done recently by the seller (we'll cover title insurance in greater detail at the end of this checklist).

Prepaid items (paid in advance at the closing):

1. Interest: If you'll keep in mind that interest is paid in arrears on a mortgage, it will make sense that the lender must charge you the interest at closing to cover the days between your closing date (June 10) and the end of the month (June 30). You then skip the July payment (since you've already prepaid the interest) and make your first official payment as a homeowner on August 1. (You can see that the later in the month you close, the less you'll have to bring to closing for prepaid interest and closing costs. Note: The lender will use 15 days of prorated interest for the purpose of estimating your Good Faith Estimate of costs.

2. Hazard insurance premium: You'll be asked to bring a paid insurance binder with you to closing. This will cover at least a one-year period and will name the lender as the loss payee. Make sure that you ask the insurance agent about securing earthquake, hurricane, and special perils insurance because most policies except these types of coverage. The lender would have notified you in advance if flood insurance from the federal government's National Flood Insurance Program is required. However, it doesn't hurt to ask how close the property is to the flood plain since you might want to secure coverage for your own peace of mind.

3. Mortgage insurance premium: As covered previously in Step #8, if you are putting less than 20 percent down, it's likely that the lender will require you to carry private mortgage insurance. You can choose to finance this up-front premium into the loan (depending on the type of plan and PMI carrier you're using) or pay this initial premium in cash at closing. In addition, you'll be asked to pay a monthly premium for the PMI insurance as well, added to your monthly PITI payment.

4. Reserve or impound account: This account accumulates in order to pay your homeowners insurance and your property taxes so you'll be asked to start the fund with a minimum one-month deposit, unless you have bargained with the lender to keep these out of the loan and pay them on your own. By law, the lender can keep no more than two months' excess in this account at any one time, with the surplus being returned to you.

Other costs on the statement:

1. Fees for a homeowners warranty (if you negotiated to pay it)
2. Home inspection fees (if you negotiated to pay them)
3. Reimbursement to the seller for early occupancy of the property (if applicable)
4. Reimbursement to the seller for any personal property you're compensating him for (could also purchase this outside of closing)

Red Flag Items to Check Out

As you review the settlement statement, be on the lookout for:

1. Costs that are charged to you that the seller agreed to pay. The closing agent uses the purchase agreement to map out who pays what. She may have made a mistake (or the purchase agreement was not clear and/or she did not interpret this charge correctly). Bring it to her attention immediately. This is one reason why reviewing the statement more than one day in advance is important!

2. Costs (particularly loan charges) that were not quoted to you initially on the Good Faith Estimate you received when you applied for the loan. While your loan needs may have changed midstream, causing you to incur more charges, you want to make sure that the lender is not "adding in a little something" that was not disclosed in the Good Faith Estimate. Charges you might find could be labeled as *warehousing fees* or *processing fees*. Question them at once. If the lender knows she's in error, they will usually be removed without further question.

3. Credits that are missing from the statement: Let's say that the seller agreed to rent the property back from you for two weeks and that credit was to appear on your closing statement. Since this is the definitive (and final) financial accounting on the property, ask where the credit is and don't close without it.

After you've reviewed (and understood) the closing statement, IT'S YOUR MOVE ♣

 Understand What Title Insurance Does and DOESN'T Do

It's a good idea to ask the closing agent for a copy of the title insurance policy to review at the same time you review the HUD settlement statement. Title insurance is a misunderstood type of insurance. And like most other types of insurance, it appears of little value until you need it! In the case of title insurance, once you need it, it's worth its weight in gold!

The title is a look to the past of all the owners, occurrences, and items of record affecting the property. That's why title insurance is best explained as insurance against future claims affecting past ownership.

Here's an example. Assume that you've owned the property for two years and one day a woman comes to your doorstep, claiming to be the owner of your house! How could you prove that she wasn't? Title insurance. It would protect and defend you against her claim of ownership.

While it might appear that claims are few and far between, you can see that when one does occur, the one-time fee of several hundred dollars that you pay for title insurance is more than justified.

A standard or basic policy is generally paid for by the seller (although this is negotiable). If you're getting a loan on the property, title insurance will also protect the lender against outside claims affecting the lender's equity in the property. And because you're the one benefiting from the loan, the lender will ask that you pay this lender's title insurance policy. This policy is called the ALTA or lender's policy.

The issue is a special concern if you're purchasing a property for which you know there's been considerable remodeling or improvements made recently. Since mechanics/workers who provide materials and labor for home improvements can file liens for nonpayment for up to several months (depending on each state's law), you might get stuck paying this unless you have a special type of title insurance to protect you. It's called extended coverage and it "extends" to cover liens that could occur after closing. (This is also suggested if you're purchasing a new home and paying cash for it since, without a lender involved, you might not have paid too much attention to the type of title insurance necessary to protect your interests. Your title company representative can advise you on this.)

Just like all other types of insurance, title insurance does not cover all circumstances. And if you're purchasing from a for-sale-by-owner and maybe using seller financing, it would be wise for your attorney to review the title insurance policy in advance of the closing. He or she could tell you what the exceptions to the coverage are, if there are any easements or other encumbrances you should be concerned about, and if any liens appear against the seller and/or the property.

If you're happy with the way the title appears (and understand what title insurance does and doesn't do), then IT'S YOUR MOVE ♣

 ## Understand What the Home Warranty Does and DOESN'T Cover

If you haven't reviewed the finite points of the home warranty plan on the property, do so now. While these may not be questions that the closing agent can answer, she should be able to get you in contact with the person who can. Again, if you close the sale (and have the warranty paid for) without getting answers to your questions, you lose your leverage and may later suffer the consequences.

Hopefully by now you've uncovered whether the warranty company is reputable and if it has the capacity to stand behind its claims. (The best-known is Home Owner's Warranty (HOW), which provides a ten-year extended warranty.) Don't assume that a warranty company is reputable just because you've heard nothing derogatory about it. Check it out with the better business bureau before the warranty is paid for.

Typical home warranty questions to find answers for include the following:

1. What is covered?
2. What are the time frames for coverage?
3. Is there a deductible amount? Does it vary by item?
4. How are claims submitted? What verification is needed?
5. Is there an appeals process if a claim is denied?
6. Most importantly (as with all types of insurance), what are the exceptions to coverage under the policy?

The last thing on your mind before you go to the closing may be reading the title insurance preliminary policy and the home warranty. But remember, you're buying peace of mind to insure against potentially expensive claims in the future. It is worth the time to understand just what you're paying for.

It looks like you're ready to have the lender answer any remaining questions you have. So IT'S YOUR MOVE ♣

Get Answers from the Lender about Your Payments and Tax and Insurance Account

If the lender is not closing the sale, you may need to talk to him/ her one last time to get answers to questions you have (unless you thought to ask them when you applied for the loan). Sometimes the closing agent may have the answers you need; other times, you'll need to make one last call to the lender.

Questions to ask the lender about your payments:

1. When is my first payment due, will I be receiving a coupon payment booklet, and is there a grace period for making the payment?
2. Are prepayments allowed on the loan? (Generally, yes, and most payment coupons have a place for noting the prepayment.)
3. If I have a question about my mortgage, whom do I call? (Most lenders will give the borrower the 800 telephone number of their loan servicer, who can answer questions about the loan.)

Questions to ask the lender about your tax and insurance impound account. If your taxes and insurance payments are part of your monthly payment:

1. How often will I get an accounting of this reserve account? (You should receive an annual accounting.)
2. How many months of reserve payments does the account have to contain? (Federal maximum requirement is two months and the overage is refunded to you annually.)
3. If I have questions about this reserve account, whom do I contact? (It may be the same number as the loan servicer, or could be a separate entity—a phone number and a physical address should be provided.)

The question to ask the lender about removing private mortgage insurance from your loan (if applicable). What are the current requirements for removing private mortgage insurance from my loan? Although these vary from lender to lender and by

loan program, general requirements most lenders follow include the following:

- The borrower must make a formal request to the lender.
- The borrower must obtain a fee appraisal showing 20 percent equity in the property.
- Monthly payments must have been paid in a timely fashion.
- PMI is removed on a case-by-case basis.

If you're happy about the answers you got from the lender, then IT'S YOUR MOVE 🔰

 ## Know Your Rights Regarding Disputes on Your Loan

We're bringing this to your attention at closing since it's good to know from the beginning that you have certain rights as a borrower under RESPA. For example, if you send a "qualified written request" (a letter outlining questions) to your loan servicer (the entity collecting your payments), that servicer must provide you with a written acknowledgment within 20 business days.

Not later than 60 business days after receiving your request, your servicer must make any appropriate corrections to your account or must provide you with a written clarification regarding any dispute. During this 60-business-day period, no adverse information about the issue can be posted with a consumer credit reporting agency. These are your rights under federal law. If you have complaints about how your inquiries were handled, you can file a complaint with HUD (Department of Housing and Urban Development) located in Washington, D.C.

There's another set of rights you need to be aware of. IT'S YOUR MOVE 🔰

 ## Know Your Rights If Your Loan Is "Sold"

"Selling the loan" typically means selling the servicing rights to the loan. It may not ever happen to your loan; yet again, it might happen several times during your loan's 30-year life. You get a letter that says, "We're writing to inform you that your loan has been sold." When that happens, you'll be glad you had this information (and this book!) to question the lender prior to closing your loan.

When the lender first gave you loan application information, part of it contained information about the likelihood of the lender selling that particular loan. It's federally mandated that both the lender saying "goodbye" to your loan as well as the one saying "hello" provide you with the following information in a timely manner.

What the "Goodbye" Lender Must Provide You

At least 15 days before the date your next payment is due, the lender selling your loan must notify you in writing and provide you (on its letterhead stationery) the name of the new company and with its full address, a phone number (800 number preferred), and the name of a contact person who can answer your questions.

What the "Hello" Lender Must Provide You

The company purchasing your loan must send you the same information in the same time frame, complete with the name of a real person (not a voice mail system) that you can speak to if you have questions.

The federal government mandated these guidelines several years ago when bogus mortgage scams had unwitting consumers rerouting their monthly payments to blind post office boxes when, in fact, their loans had never been sold. Some of the buyers found out too late—when they received loan delinquency notices from the true, original servicers of their loans!

That's why if you do not receive both the "goodbye" and "hello" letters, contact your current mortgage servicer for clarification. Federal guidelines prohibit your loan from being termed "delinquent" for a period of 60 days during the transfer of servicing. You have time to check out the facts before making any change, and don't let anyone convince you of the contrary!

If you'd like more information, an excellent free booklet is entitled "When Your Loan Is Transferred to Another Lender," available from the Mortgage Bankers Association of America, 1125 Fifteenth St., NW, Washington, DC 20005.

You did it! Congratulations! You sailed through the closing process and are ready to move into that new home! Now if you could just get someone to help you pack and move!

If you've met the eight challenges of "Pick Up Your Keys," congratulations, IT'S YOUR MOVE to Step #10 ↘

But if you've had trouble with any of the Steps, GO TO THE PENALTY BOX:

Penalty Box

Penalties could include:

1. Overpaying on your closing costs because you failed to understand items on your closing statement
2. Accepting liens and easements on your title because you didn't understand how title insurance works
3. Overpaying for several years on your private mortgage insurance because you failed to ask the lender how it could be removed from the loan

For "help" out of the PENALTY BOX:

1. Get the closing statement several days before the closing. Review it, ask the closing agent questions, and question any fees/costs that you don't understand.
2. Ask the lender what the current private mortgage insurance removal guidelines are for loans like yours and how often they do remove it from loans.
3. Know your home warranty policy in and out. Know whom to contact and how to reach this person if you do have a claim.

 Take Trump Card #9

You've come so far in the process, don't lose what you've gained by skimming over the closing statement and the documents you'll be signing. There are no silly questions where loan closing is concerned. Not questioning something you don't understand could end up costing you money!

Step

10

Manage
Your Castle

Keep It Affordable

How does it feel to be a homeowner? It's great, isn't it? No more landlords telling you what not to paint and hammer. No more rent down the drain each month.

But in addition to feeling euphoric, you may feel a little apprehensive about how you're going to keep home ownership affordable, especially if financial times get tough.

So in this final Step of the Homebuying Game, we'll pinpoint areas where you can not only save money on home ownership, but hopefully make some as well!

 Keep Your Mortgage Payments Current

It goes without saying that making your mortgage payments in a timely fashion will go a long way to creating a positive credit picture for you as well as giving you a good shot at getting another mortgage in the future.

But what if tough times hit and you find yourself unable to manage your castle financially, including being unable to meet your mortgage payment? At what point should you look for assistance? The answer: Immediately!

Although you may be a little intimidated to let the lender know you're having trouble, doing so early on can provide you with the very best chance of working satisfactorily through rough times.

Here's why. National mortgage statistics show that it can cost the lender more than 20 percent of the remaining loan balance to foreclose a property. (On a $100,000 loan, that could be as much as $20,000!) Thus, many lenders are willing to work with borrowers on a little loan forbearance to get them over tough times, such as loss of employment, medical emergency, and even divorce.

The lender can use various means to assist the borrower. For example, the lender could allow the borrower to make interest-only payments for a time, add the shortfall of payments to the back of the loan, and/or perhaps recast the loan into a more affordable mortgage. But it doesn't happen without the borrower's request—and delaying the request can lose precious time that can't be recouped.

What if the lender cannot or will not work with the borrower? Is there anything the borrower can do? Potentially. The borrower might ask the lender if he/she is willing to take a deed in lieu of foreclosure. This means that the lender forgives the borrower's debt. In turn, the borrower gives up any equity he might have in the property. But that might not be all. A deed in lieu of foreclosure might also post negatively (almost like a formal foreclosure) against the borrower's credit. And because the IRS considers it "debt forgiveness," there may be tax consequences as well! That's why a borrower should never dance lightly into a deed in lieu of foreclosure and should contact a real estate attorney as well as a tax advisor before doing so.

Are there any other options if the lender refuses to work with the borrower on a delinquency? Perhaps. If the loan is an FHA-insured loan or a VA-guaranteed loan, both government entities have workout programs to help the borrower (and the lender) out of the loan. The best way to find out if you and the loan qualify is to contact your current loan servicer for information.

The same is true of some conventional loans containing private mortgage insurance. Three of the largest PMI companies have formal workout programs to help the borrower catch up the delinquent payments and/or repay the lender those back payments, while simultaneously finding a new borrower to assume the loan and get the seller out of the picture.

What incentive would a private mortgage insurance company have to do this? The answer: a financial one. Since there would be a PMI insurance claim paid to the lender (which is often tens of thousands of dollars) due to a borrower's default, it makes much more sense for the PMI company to pay the delinquent payments to the lender than to pay a full claim.

If you try without success to get the lender to work with you on your conventional loan delinquency and you want to try the PMI workout program route, you can obtain the name of your PMI company from the payment disbursement information that appears on your loan's closing statement. Each one of the country's nine private mortgage insurance companies has a toll-free 800 telephone number. Someone in the insurance claim division should be able to assist you.

If you're geared up to keep your mortgage payments on target, then IT'S YOUR MOVE ⚓

Keep Your Property Taxes Monitored

One way to make sure that your monthly payment doesn't escalate unduly and strap you financially is to monitor your property taxes for both accuracy and fairness.

Each year, your county or municipality assesses the value of real and personal property in the county and applies a tax to it. This assessed value is reflected in the valuation notice you receive in the mail, generally several months before your tax is due.

As a taxpayer, you have the right to dispute that assessed value (thus, the corresponding property tax amount you pay). Review your assessment notice carefully and call the assessor's office about any discrepancies. Pay particular attention to the size of the property noted on the valuation form, as this is a common error that can make a difference in the tax you pay.

If you wish to protest the value, there is a specific time frame in which you can file a written complaint. If not filed by the designated date, you lose your right to appeal for that tax year.

If your taxes are under control, then IT'S YOUR MOVE

 ## Monitor and Cut Utility Bills

One way to keep your home affordable is to monitor costs and cut where you can, especially on your utilities. One of the best ways to begin the monitoring process is to have an energy audit conducted on your home. Utility and power companies in your area should have no-cost or low-cost programs in place and are an excellent, unbiased source of information, because they're typically not trying to sell you anything.

To conduct the energy audit, a technician will visit the property and perform tests on everything from furnace efficiency to insulation R-values, and determine the soundness of window treatments and the extent of heat loss in your home. (This is great information to uncover before you get ready to sell, too, since positive information—and verification—is of great interest to buyers today, as you found out!)

Once you have facts from the energy audit, you can apply them to create a more energy-efficient environment that's also cost effective. Here are some low-cost or no-cost energy efficiency tips:

1. Plant trees near the house that will provide leaves for protection against the sun in the summer, but will lose their leaves to expose the house to more sunlight in the winter.
2. Make sure that furnace ductwork is clean and that furnace filters are cleaned or replaced often. This is a low-cost item with incredible payoffs.
3. Make sure weatherstripping and caulking are tight and replaced periodically;
4. Design outdoor living centers (like decks, patios, porches) that don't require heating or cooling, but provide flexible space for extending your living space outside.

5. Turn down thermostats during winter days and heat the rooms with sunlight. In the summer, keep window coverings closed and also use white, reflective outer shades to keep sunlight from penetrating.

6. Plan meals in the summer that require little use of the stove and oven. In the winter, cook early in the morning to help warm up the house for the day (just as Grandma used to do).

7. Make sure that your water heater is set at a temperature that will heat the water, but not set so hot that it wastes energy. Wrap all exposed hot water pipes in the house with insulation.

8. Tighten dripping faucets and replace washers when worn.

Now that your utility bills are under control, IT'S YOUR MOVE 🐁

 ## Consider Low-Cost Upgrades That Make Dollars and Sense

Your energy audit showed that the house is pretty sound. But there are still some areas that you can improve on to maximize energy savings and enhance your environment.

Here are some of the top cost-effective improvements that can make dollars and sense to add to your home:

1. Install double-pane windows. While they do cost more, they can more than recoup their cost in utility bill savings.

2. Add extra insulation (especially in your attic) to trap and contain hot air rising.

3. If you have a fireplace, check to make sure the damper shuts tightly. Glass doors on the front will not only keep air from seeping into the fireplace, but will help radiate heat back into the room. Check the flashing around the top of the chimney because looseness here can cause water leakage and roof damage.

4. Insulate ductwork throughout the house to protect against air loss and keep it the proper temperature while circulating.

5. Provide storm doors to all doors. They're great for keeping inclement weather out and keeping air-conditioning in!

If the improvements you're considering are extensive and energy related, be sure to check into low-cost improvement funding offered by local housing authorities and utility companies. They may also be able to recommend contractors to do the work and/or supervise the improvements as they progress.

If you're pleased with the low-cost upgrades you've made (or will consider making), then IT'S YOUR MOVE ⬥

 ## Consider Prudent Remodeling That May Boost Your Property's Value

What if the improvements you have in mind for the house are more for the sake of enjoyment than for cost savings? It certainly doesn't make the improvements wrong. Just as with any remodeling project, they should make sense in a variety of ways based on cost-effectiveness, design and usability, and value added to the house.

So let's determine how you can evaluate that project you have in mind to see if it makes sense.

1. Avoid high-cost improvements if the value of homes has dropped or it appears that homes in the area could devalue. If you anticipate that zoning changes, alterations in traffic patterns, or other economic downturns may weaken property values, don't put money into improvements right now. Even if the area does have stable values, be sure not to overimprove the home to a much higher level than other homes in the neighborhood. It's best if your home's value is just a *little below* the best property in the area. That way you'll have room for appreciation to strengthen the property value over time, but you won't be putting money into improvements that the market won't give you credit for when you sell.

2. It's very rare to be able to recoup 100 percent of your investment in the short run when you remodel. Gather information from a real estate agent, an appraiser, and a lender before you hammer a nail. This information will help you to evaluate how your home's value fits in your neighborhood and what types of improvements will give you the best shot at affecting your property's value. This

is particularly critical if you'll be keeping the house only a short time.

3. Be sure to estimate how long you'll stay in the house after you improve it. It makes no sense to invest time and money in remodeling if you plan on moving before you derive personal satisfaction from the improvements. Ask a real estate agent to show you properties that include the improvements you're interested in, and then have him/her do a market analysis of what your home is worth right now. Economically, it may make more sense to sell now and purchase a home that's exactly what you want—without adding the expense and headache of remodeling.

4. Have any remodeling work done professionally (unless you're a Bob Vila type). No matter who does the repairs, insist on quality materials. Respect your floor plan and the layout and size of your lot. An appraiser would add only a little value for rooms that lack function and appear to be an afterthought to the general floor plan. Be sure to avoid adding rooms that are too small to be useful, poorly lit, limited in storage/closet space, and/or have limited access to other rooms in the house. Also, be sure that any remodeling plans you're considering take into regard property setbacks and easements on your lot. If you're unsure what or where these are, consult your title insurance policy and your local zoning commission/board.

5. Unless you're using cash to fund the remodeling project, don't forget to ask the lender which type of financing vehicle will be best for you to use. The logical choice might be a home equity loan, but you'll need to weigh the interest rate, costs of closing this loan, and alternative sources of financing that might be more short term and less costly.

6. The hot fix-up and remodeling areas today are the kitchen and the bathroom. Not only does remodeling add that air of "cleanliness" that is so important to both rooms, but energy and water-efficient fixtures can cut your utility costs and boost the home's resale value. And think about it—those are two rooms in the house that we spend a lot of time in!

If you've got some good ideas about what you can fix up and remodel, then IT'S YOUR MOVE ⬥

Sidestep Home Improvements That May Not Be Cost Effective

Not all home improvements (even the enjoyable ones) are wise. In fact, at times home improvements are actually detrimental to the property.

I'm reminded of a newly married couple whom I met with to list their house. They said they knew it would sell quickly, not only because it was large (four bedrooms), but they had recently spent $10,000 adding a pool in the backyard. Needless to say, the pool became a detriment when family after family of prospective buyers bemoaned, "If only this house didn't have a pool—they're so dangerous when you have little children!"

Does that mean don't add a pool? Absolutely not. It just means that in addition to being a cost-effective addition, the improvement has to be in sync with the lifestyle of the end user. (Yes, I did eventually sell the house—to another young married couple—without kids!)

Look around at other homes in the neighborhood. What features do their homes have that yours doesn't? Do any of them have the feature you're considering? Where does *that* property rate as far as market value goes? Higher or about the same as the norm?

Stay away from overimproving the property. It can be a financial "kiss of death" to be the finest castle on the block—now there's no room for the home's price to appreciate to cover the work you've done, as the price will be held down by other properties. This is often tough to detect. A quick call to your friendly real estate agent for information on some comparable homes with the amenity you're considering should help convince you which way to go.

If you do decide to make those improvements, then IT'S YOUR MOVE 🪝

 ## Be on the Lookout for Homeowner Scams

Turn on the nightly news and you're apt to see the results of unscrupulous scam artists preying on innocent homeowners. The ploys come in a wide variety of applications—everything from driveway resurfacing to bogus roof repair.

We all hope that we'll be wise enough to see through these scams. But sometimes in an effort to have work done by the lowest bidder in the shortest time, we may be duped.

Here are Red Flags to check out when working with home repair or service companies:

1. Ask to see the contractor's state licensing credentials and verification of his/her worker's compensation policy as well as proof of liability insurance coverage. It's a good idea to call the insurance company to see if the policy is still in force.

2. Check out the company with the local better business bureau (BBB), who can tell you if there's anything derogatory about the company. If the company has recently come from another locale, call the BBB in that area. Ask to see the company's (and workers', if available) credentials. These could include letters of reference, professional designations from national associations, and other credentials. Just as would be required if you were working with someone in a credit situation (which you are), ask if the company is bonded (ask to see verification); ask if it has errors and omissions insurance; and if you still have questions about its credibility, ask for a bank reference for the company.

3. Be cautious working with someone who only provides you with references for out-of-town work he's done. The same is true if he has no other local phone other than the motel down the street!

4. Run, don't walk, away from the person requiring all cash upfront or even a deposit. (Would you demand to be paid before you had rendered a service?) If the person feigns that it is to cover the purchase of materials/supplies, would you really be wise to do business with a company that is so financially unstable? Many of the signs of trouble are there initially if we'd just pay attention to them.

5. Be wary if the time for completing the job seems unrealistic (either too short or too long).

6. Your best bet in sizing up repair and home service companies is to speak directly with others who have recently used them and their services. Seeing yard signs announcing that "Ajax Concrete has recently poured a new driveway for this homeowner" is weak at best, since some unscrupulous companies actually pay homeowners to place advertising signs like that in their yards.

7. Get a minimum of three bids. If it's a costly job, six estimates is more the norm.

8. If you decide to have the work done, escrow both the funds and the repair contract with a third-party escrow holder such as the title company or attorney that closed your purchase. This way payments will only be released after the requirements of the contract are met, inspections are complete, and lien waivers signed by the workers. It's a very low-cost, low-stress way to make sure that both parties live up to their side of the bargain.

When in doubt about using a company and/or service, it's best to do nothing at all. There are very few instances when you wouldn't have ample time to first check out the people you're considering dealing with and/or be able to find another company to provide the service.

Now that we've taken care of what we're going to maintain and repair in the house, IT'S YOUR MOVE ♠

Determine How and When Prepaying Your Mortgage Makes Sense

One of the smartest ways to make your home affordable is to whittle down that 30-year loan you just signed for! Yes, you can save a few hundred dollars on your utility bills by adding weather stripping and storm doors, but if you want to save tens of thousands over the life of owning your home, start right now on a program to cut years off your mortgage!

When does prepaying your mortgage make sense?   Prepaying your mortgage may make sense for you if you identify with one or more of the following:

1. Making the mortgage payment is a financial burden. Have you had difficulty keeping up with the payments? Are you

concerned that it will mar your credit picture? Or worse yet, are you concerned that over the long run you may risk losing the property for nonpayment?

2. The interest deductibility does not have a large impact on your tax picture. While deductible interest is a nice perk, it's very rarely the reason someone would not choose to pay off a high-interest-rate mortgage.

3. A change is pending in your financial future. Based on what's going to occur (putting a child through college, funding your retirement), you realize that not having that mortgage would give you greater financial flexibility.

4. You have no plan to sell the property in the near future. This is a mistake many people make—they don't estimate how long they'll keep the property and the loan that's on it! Consequently, they use large sums of savings or investment money to pay off a mortgage only to move and need another loan! If you don't anticipate moving in the near future or refinancing into another loan, paying off this mortgage may make sense.

When does prepaying your mortgage *not* make sense?   Yes, at times prepaying your mortgage is not the best way to use your cash. See if you identify with any of these situations:

1. It would deplete financial padding should times get tough. Why would you use precious cash to pay off an interest-deductible mortgage when it would leave you without the recommended three to six months' worth of savings for emergencies? Make prepaying the mortgage just one part of your financial game plan—not the entire plan.

2. You have other high-rate nondeductible interest to pay. I'm amused when people say, "Every month, I'm prepaying a little something on my mortgage—it makes me feel much better than paying all the high interest I owe on those credit cards!" (What's wrong with this picture?) Prepaying the mortgage may make you feel better, but it makes no financial sense to do so before you've paid off that nondeductible high-rate interest on credit obligations. Once again, make prepayment part of an overall financial plan, not the sole plan.

Design a Systematic Plan for Prepaying Your Mortgage

Okay, you've weighed the pros and cons and feel that it's definitely in your financial game plan to prepay your mortgage. How do you begin? The answer: Carefully, because without a system for at least monitoring how and where your prepayments are being applied, you may come to the end of the year (or to what you think is the end of the loan) amazed at the bookkeeping errors that have occurred!

Here's why. Without proper notations, prepayments may be applied to advance interest, nonexistent late penalties, impound accounts—who knows? And because many payments are posted electronically today, these errors may actually be made by a computer. (And you know what that's like to untangle!)

So here's a systematic approach to keep your prepayment on track and your sanity intact!

When making prepayments on your mortgage, take the following steps:

1. Ask the lender (or other real estate professional, like an agent) for an amortization schedule for your loan. Your lender can provide you with a printout showing payments for the life of the loan, complete with a breakdown of principal and interest for each.

2. Choose a prepayment system that works for you. Some feel that paying a little each month is most effective since it sets a pattern (like a forced savings account). Others like to earmark their annual income tax return to pay down the loan. Whatever you choose, make sure it sets a pattern you can live with.

3. Here's a monthly program that works well. Looking at your amortization printout, you pay your January payment of $878 principal and interest. Then for your prepayment, you look ahead to the February principal reduction amount of $45.04 and you pay it. You have just prepaid the next month's principal! (See Figure 10.1.) In essence, you have eliminated one full payment from your loan since the payoff figure would correspond to the balance as of the February payment. Done systematically, you can cut years off your loan! Note that the prepayment amount

FIGURE 10.1   Mortgage Prepayment Plan

Month of Loan	Principal and Interest Payments	Interest Portion of Payment	Principal Portion of Payment	Loan Balance at End of Month
1	878.00	833.00	45.00	99,955.00
2	878.00	832.96	45.04	99.909.96
3	878.00	832.58	45.42	99,864.54
4	878.00	832.20	45.80	99,818.74
5	878.00	831.82	46.18	99.772.56
6	878.00	831.44	46.56	99,726.00
7	878.00	831.05	46.95	99,679.05
8	878.00	830.66	47.34	99,631.71
9	878.00	830.26	47.74	99,583.97
10	878.00	829.87	48.13	99,535.84
11	878.00	829.47	48.53	99,487.31
12	878.00	829.06	48.94	99,438.37

can be anything; that's why some borrowers prefer to make a set amount of prepayment monthly, say $50.

Caution: Just because you have prepaid the principal for the February payment does not mean that you don't have to *make* a February payment. Missing payments could put the loan in default—how's that for counterproductive?

4. I suggest that you make your prepayments on separate checks (be sure to list your mortgage account number on them). That way you can tally them up at year's end and make sure they've been properly applied. Be sure to mark a prepayment on your payment coupon; if none are available, mark on both the check and on a note the words, "To be applied to principal."

5. Ask the lender for an annual loan payment printout. Although you may have to make a special request, if you're making prepayments it's vital that you review your statement on an annual basis to make sure that the principal balance has been appropriately reduced.

6. When is the best time to prepay the loan? While any time is fine, prepaying in the early stages of the loan (when the majority of the payment is interest) makes the best financial sense.

Done for the right reasons (and in the correct fashion), prepaying your loan can save you thousands of dollars of interest—and give you peace of mind.

Now that we've got you whittling that mortgage down, IT'S YOUR MOVE ♣

 ## Decide How and When It Makes Sense to Tap into Your Equity

You've seen a hot tub you have to have , but your savings account is a bit sparse and your credit cards "maxed out." In general, you have "too much month at the end of the money." Then it hits you—how about borrowing against your home equity? After all, it will be a home improvement, right?

Before you tap into that precious equity, ask yourself these questions:

1. Will the item's value outlive my repayment of the debt? If the answer is "no," best to find another source of financing or wait until you can pay cash for the item.
2. Is there any other way I can finance the purchase without tapping my equity? (If you consider your equity as a last-resort resource, often you'll have second thoughts about purchasing items you really don't need in the first place.)
3. If the item is considered a home improvement, will it offset the cost I'm paying by creating added value to the property?
4. Do I need to have my home equity available for another purchase? (This is especially important if you'll be needing another loan soon that requires there be no other second mortgage on the property. In fact, some equity lenders require that all other equity lines of credit be paid off before making you a loan.)

Should You Get an Equity Line of Credit or Refinance Your Existing Loan?

Instead of refinancing your existing first mortgage, securing an equity loan (also called equity line of credit) may make economic sense. First, you don't disturb your first mortgage and can often tap up to 80 percent or more of your equity. Because equity loans are not often sold in the secondary market, many loans won't require as much documentation and paperwork as refinancing does.

However, some risks are involved with equity lines of credit. First, lenders often make them without doing a formal appraisal on the property. This could result in overleveraging (too much loan for too little value) and could be especially harmful if you need to sell the property quickly.

Second, equity lines of credit can bear higher interest rates than refinanced loans. Sometimes they contain balloon payments and are generally not assumable should you decide to sell. In fact, most equity lines will need to be paid off if you disturb the first mortgage.

That's why many homeowners, seeing financial benefit from an overall lower interest rate loan, will choose to refinance instead of taking an equity line.

If you think refinancing might be in the cards for you, then IT'S YOUR MOVE 🪶

 ## Decide If Refinancing Makes Sense

Maybe in drooling over that hot tub, you've decided that your problem might be remedied if you just refinanced your first mortgage. In fact, you might even be able to lower your monthly payment by doing so.

What *are* logical reasons to refinance? Some include being able to lower your monthly payment, shorten the term of your mortgage, and/or pay off nondeductible, high-interest debt.

Before you sign on the dotted line with the lender, have him/her prepare a financial analysis to assist you in answering the following questions:

1. What are the benefits of keeping the existing loan? (ease of loan assumability, potential for adding seller financing if the house is sold)?
2. What are the future needs for tapping equity in this property? (funding a child's education, supporting an elderly parent, funding your retirement?)
3. Would a new loan require additional costs of private mortgage insurance and/or an impound account for taxes and insurance not previously required?
4. How does the proposed loan compare with others in the marketplace based on interest rate, closing costs, and unregulated "fluff" or "garbage" fees? (If your credit rating is less than positive, you may only find refinancing by paying a premium for the new loan.)
5. How long will you keep the property and this loan? (It needs to be long enough to recoup the costs of refinancing or you've just lost money.)
6. Will cash that's pulled out of the loan be used for a sound reason that makes economic sense?

You may be thinking, "All these questions are great, but is there a basic rule of thumb that I can use to estimate if refinancing will make financial sense?" Yes, there is a rule of thumb—albeit a broad one. In general, if you can shave 2 to 3 percent interest off what you're paying now and you'll keep the property (and the loan) long enough to recoup the closing costs of refinancing, it may pay.

But (you knew this was coming, right?) it's best to pencil out a simple refinancing form to apply the numbers for your situation. (See the refinancing worksheet in Figure 10.2.)

Cautions When Deciding to Refinance

1. Shop for the best overall package. Sure, the interest rate looks great with the loan you're considering but the closing costs are high. Have the lender do financial comparisons (based on the amount of time you project keeping the loan and the property) to see which package makes the most economic sense.
2. If a lender (and/or a loan) looks too good to be true, look again. If a lender in your marketplace is touting no closing

FIGURE 10.2 Refinancing Worksheet

Would It Pay to Refinance?

A general rule of thumb is that if a borrower can shave 2 percent to 3 percent annually off interest costs, and will hold the property long enough to recoup the cost of refinancing, it may pay to refinance. Following is a chart to use in analyzing each individual situation:

Refinance Worksheet

Present Monthly Payments............. $ _____
*Number of Months to Pay.............. × _____
     Total Payments................ .$ _____ A

Payments at the Lower Rate............ $ _____
*Number of Months to Pay.............. × _____
     Total Payments................ $ _____ B
     Difference in Total Payments
     (A Minus B)................... .$ _____ C

Refinancing Costs:
     Prepayment Penalty (if applicable)$ _____ D

     Closing Costs for New Mortgage,
     including Points............... $ _____ E

     Added Income Taxes over Loan
     Term Since Reduced Deduction
     from Lower Interest............ $ _____ F

Total (D plus E plus F)............... .$ _____ G

Net Savings over Life of Mortgage (C minus G) = $ _____

*Be sure that the number of months to pay is for the period of time the borrower expects to own the property, *not* the number of months remaining on the loan.

costs, no appraisal fee, no nothing, that lender is truly the most competitive lender in town, trying to capture all of the refinance business, or she's using "free" as a smoke-and-mirrors tactic. You know the questions to ask and the numbers to compare (the same ones you asked when you got your first mortgage loan). If you don't get answers, move on down the road.

3. The lender on a refinance loan might ask if you're interested in paying more points to get a lower interest rate. Again, do the math. Just as when you made the initial decision about points on the loan you chose, do the math again. Take the amount you'd pay in extra points (e.g., $1,000) and divide it by the monthly difference between the two payments (e.g., $35). This would mean that unless you're willing to keep the property (and the loan) for more than 28 months ($1,000 divided by $35 equals 28.57 months), you'd be foolish to pay extra points. (And don't forget, this is over and above the amount you're paying for new closing costs that you've got to recoup in order to break even by refinancing!)

If you've completed the ten challenges of "Manage Your Castle"—you did it!!! You've won the Homebuying (and home-keeping) Game!

But if you had concerns with one or more of the challenges, then GO TO THE PENALTY BOX (for one last time!).

Penalty Box

Possible penalties include the following:

1. Spending thousands of dollars more on loan interest because you fail to see the wisdom in prepaying your mortgage
2. Being taken to the cleaners by unscrupulous home improvement con artists
3. Losing the house to high costs, overleveraging, and poor "castle" management

For "help" out of the PENALTY BOX:

1. Set up a strategic prepayment plan for whittling down that mortgage.
2. Do a thorough investigation of the cost-effectiveness of home improvements you're considering (and the right professionals to do them).
3. Devise a home budget and stick to it. Monitor utility costs, complete low-cost weatherization projects, and then take on cost-effective maintenance and remodeling.

 ## Take Trump Card #10

Home affordability is the key to happy, and prolonged, home ownership. But unless you keep playing those home affordability aces like weatherizing your home and whittling down your principal balance, you could end up losing what you've worked so hard to gain.

Your
Final Move!

Turn in your ten Trump Cards—
it's an unbeatable hand and worthy
of a win in the Homebuying Game!

You've done it—purchased just the right house, found a cost-effective mortgage to finance it, sailed through the closing, and are now living happily ever after in your affordable home. You've won the Homebuying Game and are to be congratulated!

The process has come full circle. In fact, you may already be dreaming of purchasing a weekend cabin or an income property. Or, heaven forbid, thinking of taking on the role of the seller to move up to that larger castle. Full circle indeed.

Whatever your real estate aspirations, I wish you luck. May you never have to replace a furnace, hear the patter of little termite feet, or (worse yet) ever have to walk away from equity! Happy home ownership!

Index